GOD'S COMFORTING WAYS

TRUE STORIES & REFLECTIONS
of GOD'S ASSURANCE

Editors of Guideposts and James Stuart Bell

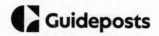

God's Comforting Ways

Published by Guideposts Books & Inspirational Media
100 Reserve Road, Suite E200
Danbury, CT 06810
Guideposts.org

ACKNOWLEDGMENTS

Every attempt has been made to credit the sources of copyrighted material used in this book. If any such acknowledgment has been inadvertently omitted or miscredited, receipt of such information would be appreciated.

Scripture quotations marked (CEV) are taken from *Holy Bible: Contemporary English Version*. Copyright © 1995 American Bible Society.

Scripture quotations marked (CSB) are taken from *The Christian Standard Bible*. Copyright © 2017 by Holman Bible Publishers. Used by permission.

Scripture quotations marked (ESV) are taken from the *Holy Bible, English Standard Version*. Copyright © 2001 by Crossway Bibles, a division of Good News Publishers. Used by permission. All rights reserved.

Scripture quotations marked (KJV) are taken from the *King James Version of the Bible*.

Scripture quotations marked (MSG) are taken from *The Message*. Copyright © 1993, 1994, 1995, 1996, 2000, 2001, 2002 by Eugene H. Peterson.

Scripture quotations marked (NASB) are taken from the *New American Standard Bible*. Copyright © 1960, 1962, 1963, 1968, 1971, 1972, 1973, 1975, 1977, 1995 by The Lockman Foundation, La Habra, California. Used by permission.

Scripture quotations marked (NIRV) are taken from *The Holy Bible, New International Reader's Version*. Copyright © 1996 by Biblica, Inc. Used by permission of Zondervan. All rights reserved worldwide. zondervan.com

Scripture quotations marked (NIV) are taken from *The Holy Bible, New International Version*. Copyright © 1973, 1978, 1984, 2011 by Biblica, Inc. Used by permission of Zondervan. All rights reserved worldwide. zondervan.com

Scripture quotations marked (NKJV) are taken from The Holy Bible, New King James Version. Copyright © 1982 by Thomas Nelson.

Scripture quotations marked (NLT) are from the Holy Bible, New Living Translation. Copyright © 1996, 2004, 2007 by Tyndale House Foundation. Used by permission of Tyndale House Publishers Inc., Carol Stream, Illinois. All rights reserved.

Scripture quotations marked (NLV) are from the *New Life Bible*, copyright © 1969 by Christian Literature International. Used by permission. All rights reserved.

Scripture quotations marked (NWT) are taken from the *New World Translation of the Holy Scriptures*. Copyright © 1961, 1984, 2013 by Watch Tower Bible and Tract Society of Pennsylvania. All rights reserved.

Scripture quotations marked (RSV) are taken from the *Revised Standard Version of the Bible*. Copyright © 1946, 1952, 1971 by the Division of Christian Education of the National Council of the Churches of Christ in the United States of America. Used by permission.

Scripture quotations marked (TLB) are taken from *The Living Bible*. Copyright © 1971 by Tyndale House Publishers, Inc., Carol Stream, Illinois. All rights reserved.

Cover design by Serena Fox
Interior design by Pamela Walker, W Design Studio
Cover photo by Shutterstock
Indexed by Kelly White
Typeset by Aptara

Printed and bound in the United States of America
10 9 8 7 6 5 4 3 2 1

CONTENTS

INTRODUCTION

BOB HOSTETLER

Pardon the expression, but the stories in this book are like manna from heaven. They whisper—and sometimes shout—sweet assurances from above that will comfort and strengthen the hearts of those who read or hear them as they did for those who first experienced them. I'm honored to introduce these pages, which include a chapter from best-selling author Don Piper, who writes about what the Bible says about heaven.

My story involves my father, who lived the last years of his life in a retirement community two miles from my home. I visited him almost daily. Each time, I would enter the facility and go straight to his room, though he was never there. I'd find him in the activity room, the chapel, or awaiting his next meal in the dining room. By his ninety-fourth year, the effects of dementia started to show up. He usually recognized my face but would ask, "Which son are you?" Otherwise, however, he had long lost all the accumulated memories of a lifetime—including my brothers and their families, his parents and siblings, and my mother, Millie, who died of breast cancer when I was a teenager. Still, as spring approached, I told my wife I thought he would live to see 100.

Then one day in March, about six weeks before his ninety-fifth birthday, I entered his facility as always, but Dad met me at the door in his wheelchair. That had never happened.

"Were you waiting for me?" I asked.

"Yes. I want to go see Millie."

His voice was strong. His eyes were clear. I don't recall what I said but I wheeled him over to the nearby table where we often worked jigsaw puzzles together. I tried to distract him, confident that he would forget all about what he had just said. But he soon returned to the subject with shocking clarity.

"Are you going to take me to see Millie?"

I explained that it was almost time for his next meal, which I knew would be a high priority for him.

"Okay, but then I want to go to Millie."

We ate lunch together, and the moment passed. He stopped pressing me to take him to see my mother. When I left, he was happily finishing his favorite dessert: chocolate pudding.

Two days later, a nurse called me from the retirement home and recommended that I arrange for hospice care, which I did. The next day, Dad slipped peacefully into eternity.

Later, as my wife, daughter, and I walked through the entrance to Dad's retirement home one last time, I slowed and then stopped. In that moment, I remembered his strange insistence on going to see Millie. I mentioned it to my wife and daughter, and again when I contacted my brothers. I later relayed it again at Dad's memorial service.

Thornton Wilder wrote in his play, *Our Town*:

We all know that *something* is eternal. And it ain't houses and it ain't names, and it ain't earth, and it ain't even the stars . . . everybody knows in their bones that something is eternal, and that something has to do with human beings. All the greatest people ever lived have been telling us that for five thousand years and yet you'd be surprised how people are always losing hold of it. There's something way down deep that's eternal about every human being.[1]

We don't see "the whole scope of God's work from beginning to end,"[2] but moments like those recounted in the pages of this book give us a glimpse. The compelling true accounts in this book, including a section of 70 devotions from everyday people who know the pain of losing a loved one, remind us that the fog that seems to separate this life and the next sometimes lifts, and we're graciously given assurances from heaven. We hope these pages will be a place you turn to daily for the kind of reflection and comfort I draw from my father's sudden urgency to "go see Millie," just days before I believe he did.

Notes:
[1]Thornton Wilder, *Our Town: A Play in Three Acts* (New York: Harper Perennial Modern Classics, 2003), 87–88.
[2]Ecclesiastes 3:11b, NLT.

PART 1

Essays

So we fix our eyes not on what is seen,
but on what is unseen, since what is seen
is temporary, but what is unseen is eternal.

—2 Corinthians 4:18 (NIV)

My Journey with Grief and God's Goodness

ISABELLA CAMPOLATTARO

I will not leave you comfortless: I will come to you.
John 14:18 (KJV)

I've faced more grief than most people my age. At 53, I've lost both parents, an important father figure, all my grandparents, my older brother, several aunts and uncles, and three dogs. Each loss was different, eliciting an altogether different grief journey. The nature of the relationship, my spiritual maturity, the circumstances, were all factors that influenced my experiences. God's comfort met me where I was.

My brother's untimely death at twenty-five was my first encounter with loss and by far the most agonizing for several reasons. Perhaps that's why God graciously dispensed supernatural comfort. My mother's death at eighty-three after an intensely tragic life and difficult passing was different. I felt gentle relief at the prospect of her eternal peace. My charismatic alcoholic father's death pierced me, but I was detached, even numb, after grieving our damaged relationship while he was alive. I barely knew three of my four grandparents, who were already quite old when I was born and an ocean away in Italy, as were my aunts and uncles. So very different, each one.

I've found that God often reveals Himself most personally when I'm suffering, particularly in navigating the difficult terrain of death.

God's Comforting Ways

Praise be to the God and Father of our Lord Jesus Christ, the Father of compassion and the God of all comfort, who comforts us in all our troubles, so that we can comfort those in any trouble with the comfort we ourselves receive from God.
2 Corinthians 1:3–4 (NIV)

Grieving is so intense and intimate, only our Heavenly Father's loving hand can penetrate the deep darkness. Laid bare in our sorrow, He alone knows everything about us, about our griefs. He alone promises to comfort us with compassion. God's comforting ways are as varied as the experience of grief. I've experienced or witnessed God's loving comfort in

- **The universality of grief.** There is comfort in knowing that mourning is common to humankind because of its inevitability for all of us.

> *He alone knows everything about us, about our griefs.*

- **Being one with Christ.** We can find solace in knowing we share the heart of Father, Son, and Holy Spirit, all of whom have known grief.
- **Knowing we're destined for eternity.** Our grief is both magnified and tempered by the knowledge that heaven is our eternal home.

- **Feeling homesick.** Because heaven is our eternal home, it's only natural that we'd be homesick, and in that, to know we'll one day join our loved ones in heaven.
- **Messengers of peace.** God sometimes dispatches mysterious ambassadors of hope, sometimes people who truly seem like angels of mercy.
- **Gentle warnings.** Some of us experience foretelling dreams that prepare us for what's to come, reminding us that God— and our loved ones—are outside of time.
- **Apparitions and dreams.** Our heavenly Father is not limited by this dimension and can comfort with otherworldly images of loved ones or glimpses of heaven itself.
- **Signs of peace.** Symbolic comforts that signal the love and safety of our loved ones bring peace.
- **Comforting connections.** A simple phone call or unexpected connection can be a great solace at a difficult time.

God's comfort is as unique as the loss itself but bound together by the universality of the experience.

The Universality and Uniqueness of Grief

Blessed are those who mourn, for they shall be comforted.
Matthew 5:4 (ESV)

Grief is remarkably common, and knowing that is comforting. A 2019 WebMD.com and AmeriSpeak study[3] found that at any given time, 57 percent of Americans are grieving the loss of a loved one. Still, grief is profoundly individual, though with many shared aspects that unify the experience for most of us. Only those who have experienced grief in all its variations can truly understand how profound, shattering, and even surreal it can be. Elisabeth Kübler-Ross's[2] familiar five stages of grief—denial, anger, bargaining, depression, and acceptance—offer a simple framework to help us understand the grieving process. But the reality is more complex.

The same study describes how varied the intensity, duration, and experience of grief can be. People can suffer sadness, depression, or painful obsession about the loss. When my brother Rick died, I felt a searing pain I can't describe and was haunted by his memory for years, sometimes blindsided by tears for no apparent reason. Some people feel anger, bitterness, denial, or numbness as I did when my dad died. Many experience profound fatigue. For most of us, grief causes a mysterious yet achingly familiar swirl of all these feelings, sometimes shifting suddenly. I've gone from laughing wistfully to choking on my own tears in moments.

> *Grief causes a mysterious swirl of feelings, sometimes shifting suddenly.*

In his seminal and vulnerable work on the subject, *A Grief Observed,* C. S. Lewis wrote poignantly about the unpredictability of grief after the loss of his adored wife.

> For in grief nothing "stays put." One keeps on emerging from a phase, but it always recurs. Round and round. Everything repeats. Am I going in circles, or dare I hope I am on a spiral? But if a spiral, am I going up or down it? How often—will it be for always?—how often will the vast emptiness astonish me like a complete novelty and make me say, "I never realized my loss till this moment"? The same leg is cut off time after time.

It's interesting that the study also noted that only 31 percent sought out faith or spiritual practices to cope with the effects of loss. When my brother Rick died of a drug overdose, I drew away from God, but not because I was angry. I'd tried to help Rick get clean for years. I remember praying desperately night after night that God would alleviate Rick's suffering.

When he finally died in his own bed after a deadly cocktail of pills, I immediately sensed that God had answered my prayer. It was an agonizing answer, but unmistakably clear. Though the grief was immediate and intense, that revelation gave me a measure of relief. I imagined Rick like the thief on the cross, crying out to Christ in desperate recognition, and Jesus responding with brotherly eternal comfort (Luke 23:42–43). A comfort I still share with others in keeping with God's intent described in 2 Corinthians 1:4.

Pastor Rick Warren, who lost his own son to suicide, said this: "Surrender is when you say I'd rather live and walk with God and have my questions unanswered than have all my questions answered and not walk with God."[3]

I simply choose to believe that God's compassion for us is unfailing, and He demonstrates His loving sovereignty in this broken world where death exists.

Paternal Compassion and the Man of Sorrows

> *The LORD is close to the brokenhearted and*
> *saves those who are crushed in spirit.*
> Psalm 34:18 NIV

I believe God's comforting ways are informed by something more than His omniscience and infinite love. God the Father, Son, and Holy Spirit all know grief.

In Genesis 6:6, God is grieved by the mess we made of Creation as only a dad can be, and Ephesians 4:30 (NIV) warns us not to "grieve the Holy Spirit of God." I sense this grief is like any parent's heartbreak when their child makes self-destructive choices.

Our brother and Savior knew the pain of loss, too. Isaiah 53:3 (NLT) describes Jesus as "a man of sorrows, acquainted with deepest grief." John 11:35 (NIV) tells us that "Jesus wept" at the loss of his dear friend Lazarus. In His humanity, Jesus

> *His comfort is a reflection of His very human experience of pain.*

felt the agony of loss. His comfort is a reflection of His very human experience and understanding of pain, coupled with His deeply personal relationship with each of us.

Sharing in His Suffering and His Glory

> *Be glad for the chance to suffer as Christ suffered.*
> *It will prepare you for even greater happiness*
> *when he makes his glorious return.*
> 1 Peter 4:13 (CEV)

God comforts us by assuring us that in the depth of mourning, we share both in Christ's suffering and, eventually, in His eternal glory. In Ephesians, Paul prays for us to know God, to grasp the extent of His love, and to see clearly the eternal hope we have in Him and "the power he worked in Christ when he raised him from the dead and seated him at his right hand in the heavenly places" (Ephesians 1:15–20 and Ephesians 3:14–21, ESV). There are many such references to assure us of eternal glory. An eternal glory we earn partly by sharing in the pain of the cross (Romans 8:17).

In *A Path Through Suffering*,[4] Elisabeth Elliot, widow of missionary Jim Elliot, who was killed by Ecuadoran Huaorani natives, and
who lost two other husbands to untimely deaths, wrote this:

"The place where we must meet Him today is the cross where the
Lord of the Universe dealt finally with death," adding, "It is no vague
and silly optimism we speak of, no false mysticism…(page 128)."

Elsewhere, Elliott declares, "We have our Father's promise,
linking the pain to an unimaginable glory" (page 45).

Designed for Eternity

They are not of the world, just as I am not of the world.
John 17:16 (ESV)

I believe one of the reasons grief is such a profound experience is
that we weren't meant to die. We're designed for eternity. Thus, in
facing death, on some deep level our own spirits are burdened by
a longing for heaven. When God breathed life into Adam (Genesis
2:7, ESV) and formed Eve from his rib (Genesis 2:21–22, ESV), He
intended that they would rule over creation, enjoying a perfect paradise and God's loving companionship forever. With the Fall came
death, the ultimate consequence and a looming threat that forever
haunts most people, faithful or otherwise. Remembering our eternal
zip code can bring great consolation.

In Scripture, we're told that as Christians, we're not of this world.
Most notably, Jesus mentions our otherworldliness Himself several
times in the book of John, repeatedly reminding his disciples that
like Him, we aren't of this world (John 15:19, 17:14, 17:16, and
18:36). I'd never noticed how emphatic Jesus is on this powerful
point. Surely, anything Jesus repeats so forcefully is something we
should take very much to heart. My own fresh reading of these

verses offered new perspective. Earthly woes, including loss, *do* seem less terminal in light of our eternal citizenship. Even so, holding onto the truth of eternity is admittedly difficult in the face of our current realities, mired in this concrete realm we experience with our senses.

> *Earthly woes seem less terminal in light of our eternal citizenship.*

God knows this and loves us, so through the voices of Scripture, He repeatedly encourages us to "set [your] minds on things that are above, not on things that are on earth" (Colossians 3:2 ESV). As Paul says euphorically in 2 Corinthians 4:17–18 (ESV),

> For this light momentary affliction is preparing for us an eternal weight of glory beyond all comparison, as we look not to the things that are seen but to the things that are unseen. For the things that are seen are transient, but the things that are unseen are eternal.

I reach for this reality anytime I suffer, remembering that whatever joys and sorrows I face here are short-lived, and what awaits us and loved ones in heaven far outweighs even our most searing losses here.

Homesick

*I*n Philippians, a book commonly known as the joy letter, God graces Paul with more palpable eternal perspective on the promise of Heaven. Simply put, we're homesick. In verse 3:20 Paul reminds the Philippian faithful that "our citizenship is in heaven" and that ultimately, Jesus will "transform our lowly bodies to be like His glorious body" (Philippians 3:21, ESV). Indeed, Paul reminds us that the human body is subject to destruction, and that "we grow weary in our present bodies, and we long to put on our heavenly bodies like new clothing" (2 Corinthians 5:2, NLT).

Could it be that grief is magnified by our weariness of this broken world, these broken bodies? Maybe we are unconsciously "groaning" for "the day when it will join God's children in glorious freedom from death and decay" (Romans 8:21–22, NLT). By God's grace, I've gratefully enjoyed this conviction in the face of intense heartache.

This side of heaven, our bodies fail us, but beyond this earth, we—like our loved ones—will have heavenly bodies, free of sickness and decay. It's comforting to know these defective mortal vessels will be replaced by eternal bodies. We can join Paul in proclaiming, "O death, where is your victory? O death, where is your sting?" (1 Corinthians 15:55 NLT).

By the time Mamma died in 2014, I'd been a passionate Christian for nearly fifteen years. I had loved Mamma almost unto my own death. Brilliant, charming, and fascinating, Mamma was also an erratic paranoid schizophrenic and had suffered greatly. It was painful to love her, and I'd grieved her even as she lived. This fact, coupled with my certainty of a tearless heaven, enabled me to let her go with peace and even joy. It was a great comfort to imagine her reunited with my brother, her parents, and Jesus, restored to her physical beauty and mental wholeness.

Messengers of Comfort

Don't forget to show hospitality to strangers, for some who have done this have entertained angels without realizing it!
Hebrews 13:2 (NLT)

*I*n Hebrews, we learn that angels can come to us undercover—ambassadors from God—to inform, guide, and yes, comfort us. Appearing throughout scripture, reassuring angels were dispatched to Zechariah to announce the birth of John the Baptist (Luke 1:13 NLT), to Mary for the Annunciation (Luke 26–37 NLT), and to Joseph to encourage him to embrace his unexpected mission without fear (Matthew 1:20 NLT). While we readily accept human fascination with angels revealed in popular television shows and household decor, when we have inexplicable encounters in times of sorrow, we may hesitate to accept that we've truly had a helpful heavenly encounter.

> *Angels can come to us undercover to inform, guide, and comfort us.*

My friend Tammy lost her twenty-nine-year-old first husband, Barry, to melanoma. Twenty years later, happily remarried, she still has vivid memories. Barry was in the final stages of his fight, bedridden in the guest room of his childhood home where his mom, Carol Anne, a nurse, was helping to care for him. While preparing food for him, the two women were startled by a knock on the door. There stood an older man who introduced himself as John. Neither women had ever seen him before.

John explained he knew Barry from their neighborhood dog walks and asked to speak to him. Both Tammy and Carol Anne were skeptical, but something compelled Tammy to ask Barry if he was willing. Equally surprising, he was open to meeting John, who prayed over Barry alongside Tammy. John's prayer and presence were inexplicably comforting and a seemingly direct answer to Tammy's anguished cries to God just hours before.

Later, over coffee in the kitchen, John shared Scripture with Tammy that blessed her with deep peace and even joy. Another answer to her heartfelt morning plea. As he left, John warned that Barry didn't have much time.

Hours later, Barry took his last breath with Tammy at his side. Neither Tammy nor Carol Anne ever saw John again.

Death Foretold: Preparing the Way

A person's days are determined; you have decreed the number of his months and have set limits he cannot exceed.
Job 14:5 (NIV)

Prophecy, is of course, a common theme in all of our Scripture, including prophetic dreams and other prophecies about the exact circumstances of Jesus's own death. In His sovereign mercy, God sometimes allows us to glimpse a future loss that later can provide comforting wonder at God's kindness and timelessness.

Tammy told me that years before Barry was diagnosed, she had recurring dreams that proved to be premonitions. In one dream, a group of young men in crisp white shirts and ties were standing in a group at what seemed to be a funeral, mournfully saying, "So young" and "Just twenty-nine." In another similar dream, it was a group of elderly women, murmuring sadly, "Only thirty." The dream was so vivid it became a running joke between Tammy and Barry, up until Tammy's twenty-ninth birthday only months before Barry's death. Unaware of his fate, Barry teased Tammy that she'd turned thirty and was still alive. After Barry's death, Tammy recalls finding the prophetic dreams a reassurance of another realm.

Glimpses of Heaven

After this I saw a vast crowd, too great to count, from all nations
and provinces and languages, standing in front of the throne and
before the Lamb, clothed in white, with palm branches in their hands.
Revelation 7:9 (TLB)

We've all heard stories of the dying seeing beloved loved ones beckoning from beyond, ushering them into heaven. Apart from the many poetic glimpses offered by John the Revelator, Scripture assures us we'll see recognizable figures in heaven. Matthew 8:11 tells us we'll recline with the likes of Abraham, Isaac, and Jacob, so we can be confident of our reunions with those who go before us. And in Luke 16:22 (NIV), we're told that a beggar died "and the angels carried him to Abraham's side." My friend Kathleen's experience is an uncanny illustration of both divine transportation and heavenly welcome.

> *Scripture assures us we'll see recognizable figures in heaven.*

Kathleen's mom, Lena Pioggia, was eighty-three when she was admitted to the hospital with pneumonia. Even though Mama had COPD, Kathleen and her sisters, nurses Linda and Peggy, didn't fear the worst. Their mom was a fighter and her devoted daughters never left her side. But the pneumonia took its toll, eventually causing serious cardiac issues. The daughters kept encouraging their mom through endless days of relentless poking, testing, and battling to breathe.

After three weeks, a weary Lena quietly confessed to Kathleen, "I'm tired, honey. I can't do this anymore."

She wanted to be moved to the hospital's hospice unit. Heartbroken, the sisters recognized their mom was at peace with her decision, and they couldn't argue with her. They reluctantly agreed but struggled with letting their mother go. Lena's large Italian family came to say goodbye and the sisters wept in despair at losing their treasured Mama. Then she started calling for her own mother, in a peaceful, hopeful, almost childlike tone. Was she seeing her mother? the sisters wondered. Even then, the pain at letting her go was too great.

A nurse gently suggested that maybe her mother was reluctant to die because her daughters hadn't surrendered. She urged them to go pray in the chapel. The trio cried out loud for God to help them have the courage to surrender their mother as she had surrendered herself. An hour later, peacefully spent, they returned to their mother's room. The feeling was different.

"I knew she was going to go and that it would be okay," Kathleen remembers. The sisters circled the bed murmuring lovingly, when suddenly Peggy, the youngest, said "She's gone." Kathleen and Linda confirmed their mom had drawn her last breath and turned to Peggy, curious. That's when Peggy excitedly explained that she'd felt a presence nearly shove her out of the way.

"It felt like they lifted her right out of the bed and carried her out." *Who were "they"? Angels?*

Whoever or whatever, the experience was a tangible comfort for the three grieving sisters.

Assuring Apparitions and Dreams

And there appeared before them Elijah and Moses, who were talking with Jesus.
Mark 9:4 (NIV)

*D*reams and visions abound in the Bible and may remain one of the most common forms of divine communication and comfort in grief. Daniel, for instance, was a prophetic dreamer endowed with the ability to interpret dreams (1:17; 2:28 NLT). Tellingly, the Bible frequently seems to use the terms *dreams* and *visions* interchangeably, suggesting that the line between the two is blurred. This seems to bear out in real-life experience, including my own.

I was just nineteen when my brother Rick died at twenty-five of an accidental overdose. He'd battled substance abuse for more than a decade—an addiction I believe was spurred by mental illness. He was sometimes deeply depressed, paranoid, and erratic, always struggling. Even though our relationship had been difficult, I adored Rick, and the sting I felt at Rick's death stunned me.

> *Rick looked at me and said in a gentle voice, "I'm okay," and promptly vanished.*

The night of Rick's death, in the small hours, I lay sleepless on the living room sofa. My heartache was so intense that my whole body felt heavy with the weight of it. Suddenly, Rick appeared before me, only a few feet away. He was ghostlike, a sheer specter, but vivid, dimensional, real. I was at once surprised and peaceful and not the least bit afraid. Rick looked me squarely in the face and said in a gentle voice, "I'm okay," and promptly vanished. I've never experienced that again and believe God graced me with the comforting image at a particularly difficult time in my life.

Apart from Elijah and Moses's appearance at the Transfiguration, the Bible speaks openly about spirits and other references of the resurrected dead appearing to others. Of course, most memorably, the resurrected Jesus Himself appeared before His disciples in the locked upper room (John 20:19). Matthew 27:52–53 (NIV) says "many holy people were raised to life" when Jesus died on the cross, appearing "to many people" in Jerusalem.

Even in the nearly delirious stupor that early grief can sometimes be, I believe I saw Rick in a supernatural form.

On the other hand, my brother Dario has received comfort in the form of several vivid dreams of Rick, and later, of our father and our surrogate father. In one early dream, Rick appeared unexpectedly.

Dario remarked, "Oh, I thought you were gone," and Rick responded with a chuckle, saying "No, I'm here."

Dario admits those early dreams of Rick were tangibly comforting in the moment but then later deeply disappointing when Rick wasn't alive after all. In contrast, similar dreams of our father and surrogate father were happy dreams that left a lasting and pleasant sense of nostalgia.

In telling me his dream stories, Dario casually said, "Maybe God put them in my dream."

This immediately resonated with my spirit. It would be so like our loving God to gift us with joyful images of departed loved ones, carefully "placing them" in our dreams.

Signs of Peace and Comfort

And when Jesus was baptized, immediately he went up from the water,
and behold, the heavens were opened to him, and he saw the Spirit of
God descending like a dove and coming to rest on him.

Matthew 3:16 (ESV)

The Bible is full of signs and symbols that convey rich meaning, so it seems logical that sometimes mystical signs we encounter when we lose a loved one are real and true. Jesus's own death is both foreshadowed and remembered with signs, including the lamb (John 1:29 ESV), the scapegoat (Leviticus 16:8 ESV), and bread and wine (1 Corinthians 11:23–27 ESV). And of course, the cross reminds of both Christ's death and His resurrection.

My friend Lisa Ortega's son Michael took his own life last year after a long struggle with mental illness and addiction. Moments after she heard the unbearable news, she called her sister Susan, who was sitting on Clearwater

The Bible is full of signs and symbols that convey rich meaning.

Beach with her boyfriend, Brian. Susan gasped, tearfully describing how she and Brian, both devoted pelican rescue volunteers, had just been watching a pelican conspicuously frolicking in the waves before them, playing and splashing joyfully.

"It was Michael!" Susan exclaimed.

Lisa and Susan both recalled how an exotic bird had appeared to her father and stepmom at the death of her treasured step-grandmother—so it was family lore Michael knew well.

Similarly, my friend Kathleen told me how her sister Peggy found a penny tucked under her keyboard soon after her mama Lena died.

Their mom would say "pennies from heaven" any time she found a penny and, later, upon seeing a white butterfly, a sign associated with her son Robert, who'd died suddenly at forty.

Now anytime they see a penny, the sisters rejoice at the memories of their beloved mother and brother.

Birds are a common symbol of comfort for the grieving. My friend Angie first experienced this comfort while she was going through chemotherapy, uncertain of her own survival. Always a spiritual seeker, the illness led to what Angie calls a deep dive with her faith. Nature was a special comfort, and especially birds.

So when her brother Billy died just months ago, she was tuning in to nature to alleviate not only her own grief but also the anguish of seeing her mother and her niece and nephew suffer inconsolably. On one particularly difficult day, Angie, fraught with anxiety, stepped away from her desk to clear her head. Just as she walked into her kitchen, she saw a bright red cardinal fly quickly from her backyard fence to the lanai screen. By now spiritually attuned to God's ways, she immediately knew it was a sign.

Five Ways God Comforts Us

1. **Messengers of Peace:** God sometimes sends angels of mercy and ambassadors of hope.
2. **Gentle Warnings:** God can grant us a prophetic glimpse of a loved one's imminent death, reminding us of his timeless sovereignty.
3. **Apparitions & Dreams:** God comforts with otherworldly images of loved ones or glimpses of heaven itself.
4. **Signs of Peace:** God can infuse familiar creatures or objects with symbolic meaning that tell us our loved ones are with Him.
5. **Comforting Connections:** God inspires people to connect with us in a meaning-filled, comforting way.

"I truly believe that was God saying, 'Focus here,'" she recounts. "Billy's okay, you're okay, everyone will be okay."

The cardinal clung there, almost as if to say, "Hey, look at me," she remembers.

As she became calmer, the bird flew back to the nearby fence. When she was fully serene, the cardinal flew off.

Angie finds these natural messengers appear most obviously when things seem darkest.

God does seem nearest to us when we are most bereft, but God is always close. We're the ones who draw near to Him when we're sorrowing.

Comforting Connections

Praise be to the God and Father of our Lord Jesus Christ, the Father of compassion and the God of all comfort.
2 Corinthians 1:3 (NIV)

Not all of us experience supernatural manifestations of God's comfort, but many see God work through the people in our lives as we mourn. Jesus said loving one another is second only to loving Him (Matthew 22:39 NIV). The simple comfort of a well-attended wake can remind us we are loved and our loved one is remembered. Sharing tears with others can alleviate the burden of grief. Other times, it's a timely phone call or thoughtful note that penetrates the darkness of grief.

As Lisa suffered the unbearable questions after Michael's suicide, his girlfriend called, explaining she had a persistent sense she had to call Lisa to tell her she was a good mom. Lisa admits she needed to hear that.

Sharing tears with others can alleviate the burden of grief.

Three Verses to Carry in Your Heart

He will wipe away every tear from their eyes, and death shall be no more, neither shall there be mourning, nor crying, nor pain anymore, for the former things have passed away.
Revelation 21:4 (ESV)

He is close to the brokenhearted and saves those who are crushed in spirit.
Psalm 34:18 (NIV)

And even we Christians, although we have the Holy Spirit within us as a foretaste of future glory, also groan to be released from pain and suffering. We, too, wait anxiously for that day when God will give us our full rights as his children, including the new bodies he has promised us—bodies that will never be sick again and will never die.
Romans 8:23 (TLB)

The Promise of Heaven

He will wipe away every tear from their eyes, and death shall be no more, neither shall there be mourning, nor crying, nor pain anymore, for the former things have passed away.
Revelation 21:4 (ESV)

However our loving Father comforts us in mourning lost loved ones, our ultimate hope rests on the promise of an eternity in a place where "No eye has seen, no ear has heard, and no mind has imagined what God has prepared for those who love him" 1 Corinthians 2:9 NLT.

Some, like Don Piper, have glimpsed the promise that awaits all of us, as you will see on the next pages.

Heaven's Majesty

DON PIPER

One of the most remarkable discoveries we make in life is death. Not long after we arrive on the planet, we are shocked to find out we do not get to stay. Our grandpa passes away. A classmate is killed in a tragic accident. We're confronted with a stark reality. The death rate here is 100 percent. *We* are part of this statistical certainty.

For most of us the obvious question follows: What happens after life on earth? Since we are very much alive while we're asking this question, we want to know if there is something beyond this life. Who do we turn to for answers?

For all of us, our first communication with God is through prayer. And it is in turning our thoughts toward the firmament that we begin to understand. Consider the words Jesus gave to his disciples when they asked how to pray. The Lord's Prayer, quite simply, is heavenly. From its first words we hear this affirmation, "Our Father which art in heaven" (Matthew 6:9 KJV). Jesus is saying that while He was physically in our presence when He uttered these words, God the Father resided in heaven . . . a completely different place.

As the magnificent words of the prayer unfold, we hear "Thy Kingdom come. Thy will be done, in earth as it is in heaven"

(Matthew 6:10, KJV). There's that word again. *Heaven*. Jesus, the Son, is talking to God, the Father, in the place where God is, heaven.

So, what and where is heaven? What happens there? Can *we* go there—and when?

Has Heaven Always Existed?

This question implies there was a time before heaven existed. If that is true, where did God dwell? We must first look at time itself. Genesis begins with these three words, "In the beginning." We could easily conclude that before this creation moment, there was no time. Even time is a creation of God. He certainly doesn't live in time constraints. My contention is that God has always existed. Everything that followed is His creation, including time. So even heaven is a creation of God, and it was created at a specific time, "In the beginning."

> God wants us in heaven with Him. That's why He created it.

Heaven is about hope—today and tomorrow. Maybe many tomorrows. You might not take your last earthly breath for many earthly years. You might take your last breath tonight. Knowing where we are going when we leave this planet should have a powerful effect on how we live our lives on the way there. We can live with confidence, determination, and assurance. God wants us in heaven with Him. That's why He created it. And God earnestly desires that we have a better journey on the way there.

The love, the joy we'll feel when we're in heaven is beyond anything we experience here on earth. I've seen it with my own eyes.

Experiencing Heaven

I was driving across a narrow bridge over the Trinity River when an eighteen-wheeler slammed into me head-on. I was declared dead by four paramedics at the scene. And I remained dead for an hour and a half. Upon dying, I did not journey down a long tunnel toward a bright light as many have experienced. For me a one-hundred-ten miles an hour earthly impact between my car and the truck meant I was immediately at the gates of heaven.

Since that landmark event I've met many people who have traveled down a tunnel to the dazzling light upon death. I believe that experience of dying is more common simply because more people pass from this life gradually than in sudden accidents.

I found myself enveloped in the light of heaven at one of heaven's twelve gates. Yes, according to Revelation 21:21 (KJV), there are twelve gates in heaven. This gate in heaven looked like the inside of an oyster . . . mother of pearl. Iridescent, luminescent, shimmering, and brilliantly white.

The most matchless sight beheld at the gates was my loved ones who had preceded me in death. Aunts, uncles, teachers, classmates, neighbors, dear friends, mentors, and grandparents greeted me with expansive smiles and open arms. Beautifully attired in dazzling robes, they were obviously expecting me.

In heaven, I believe, there are no strangers. The Bible provides several examples of people who had never met on earth nonetheless recognizing each other after death. Luke 16:19–31 offers a powerful parable in which a man on earth recognizes a person he knew named Lazarus (not the one raised from the dead by Jesus) in heaven in addition to his own brothers in heaven. The apostle Peter knew Moses and Elijah as they appeared with Jesus on the Mount of Transfiguration, even though Peter and those two saints were not contemporaries. They died centuries before Peter.

At center stage for my blessed arrival was my dear grandfather, "Joe Sox" Kulbeth. I rode in the ambulance with him the night he had a massive heart attack. The kindly old doctor's eyes glistened as he informed me Papa had passed away. When Papa died, it broke my heart. Seeing Papa as he greeted me at heaven's gate healed my heart and filled it with joy.

> *Seeing Papa as he greeted me at heaven's gate filled my heart with joy.*

Much of the communication in heaven is not spoken audibly. But Papa extended his arms to me and said in a language I had never heard before but fully understood, "Welcome home, Donnie!" (Donnie was his pet name for me on earth. In adulthood, no one else called me by that name.)

My great-grandparents, J. R. and Hattie Mann, greeted me there as well. As a kid visiting them in Monticello, Arkansas, each trip began and ended on their front porch on Godbold Street. At heaven's gates, we were meeting again, this time on God's front porch. What a spectacular reunion it was! 1 Thessalonians 4:17–18 (NIV) offers this exciting truth, "And so we will be with the Lord forever. Therefore encourage each other with these words."

Every one of the people who met me at the gates of heaven was someone who had contributed to my coming to Christ on earth. These souls had taken me to church because I had no other way to go, given me Bibles because I didn't own one, told me about Jesus because I didn't know about Him, and lived faithful lives in front of me so I'd know what a Christian was meant to be. Yes, they helped me get to heaven. And now they were greeting me upon my arrival.

I was home. Heaven really is home.

Sights, Sounds, and Smells

My most vivid memory of my time in heaven was the music that never ends. When I tell people about my experience, many are surprised that my most enduring heavenly recollection was not something I saw but what I heard: music. I heard things, but none rose to the awesome thrill of music sung, played, and offered to Almighty God Himself.

God is the audience of all authentic worship. The glorious music in heaven takes many forms, but all of it praises God. Anthems, praise songs, hymns, spirituals, choruses, cymbals, horns, harps, flutes, songs of the saints and angels and us! I could not only hear the angels sing, I could also hear their wings flapping. What a comforting, majestic sound that was. Thousands of songs rendered simultaneously, without chaos. All the music was symbiotic—it fit together seamlessly. Where else could that happen but heaven?

Praise and worship in heaven are ceaseless. I want to hear that music once more. My nature is and has always been musical. How splendid is the music of heaven? I want *you* to hear it. *God* wants you to hear it.

Heaven has its own sweet aroma. One of the smells of heaven is the aroma of the prayers of the saints wafting from the throne of God. Revelation 5:8 tells us that "the twenty-four elders fell down before the Lamb, each holding a harp and golden bowls full of incense, which are the prayers of the saints" (ESV). Even now, our prayers are permeating the throne of God, and their sweet smell, no matter how desperate or painful the prayer, is a fragrance that floats from the throne of God.

Consider the sights of heaven I encountered. First, brilliant light, and then a glorious gate and "welcoming committee" of family and friends who helped me get there. Then I saw the walls, which are 216 feet thick, 1,500 miles high, and 1,500 miles by 1,500 miles square or 2.25 million square miles. There is a street of pure gold that is transparent (Revelation 21:21), a tree of life from which we can eat (Revelation 2:7 and 22:2), a river of life from which we drink (Revelation 22:1), rooms for each child of God (John 14:2), and a throne (Isaiah 6:1; Revelation 4:2; 2 Chronicles 18:18; Psalm 11:4). As astonishing as these physical elements of heaven are, they aren't even the best thing about heaven.

> *The glorious music of heaven takes many forms, but all of it praises God.*

Here's the very best thing about heaven: God will dwell *among us*. Revelation 21:3 tells us three times that He will be with us. It's His place, and we will be with Him!

Conversely, some things are *not* found in heaven, and when you see the list it might surprise you! Sin, death, mourning, crying, pain, night, church, corruption, the sun or moon, Satan, or a sea because on earth, seas separate us from each other.

Jesus and Heaven

Reflect on Philippians 2:6–8 (NIV): *Who, being in very nature God, did not consider equality with God something to be grasped, but made himself nothing, taking the very nature of a servant, being made in human likeness. And being found in appearance as a man, He humbled himself and became obedient to death—even death on a cross!*

Jesus's departure from heaven brought about a great deal of emotional distress between God, the Father, and Jesus, the Son. The Bible reveals they were in virtually constant communication the entire time Jesus was on earth. Though utterly divine, Jesus, in His humanity, even asked to be spared from the horror of crucifixion and pleaded with God as He agonized in the Garden of Gethsemane. The earthly mission of Jesus was clear from His advent: to save people from their sins and definitively establish a permanent relationship with humans. It had become obvious that humans were not going to obey the laws God had given us. A *way* to bridge that chasm between a holy God and sinful humans was imperative. Jesus identified himself as *"the way, the truth, and the life."*

Only God knows what the absence of Jesus from heaven was like for those 33½ earthly years. Since heaven is a timeless place, perhaps Jesus's time on earth was but a twinkle in the eye of God in heaven.

Jesus had to feel alone and even sometimes abandoned while he walked this planet. "My God, my God, why have you forsaken Me?" (Matthew 27:46 NASB). His performance of miracles, His life-altering words, His deep love for His friends and followers, His deep love for those who ridiculed and even killed Him would mean God knows us intimately. And Jesus's presence here with us should mean we know Him.

Jesus's life, death, and resurrection changed everything. "I go to prepare a place for you," Jesus said (John 14:2 KJV). Who better than a carpenter King to build us a better place?

Finding Comfort in Grief

As incredible as heaven is, for those of us left here on earth after a loved one passes, the sorrow can be devastating. We can't help but miss the company of our friends and family. Death can leave us searching for meaning in our lives. How do we find comfort in the assurance of heaven?

> *As incredible as heaven is, we can't help but miss the company of those who have passed on.*

A few years ago, a man I didn't know named Phil left a message on my office phone. It was hard to understand his words. He was trying to hold it together but not succeeding. What did come through was that he wanted to talk to me.

I called Phil. He lived about seventy miles from Houston where I live. He sounded younger than he probably was. I heard a baby crying in the background.

He shared his story. His wife had died suddenly only three weeks before. But that wasn't nearly all of it. She had given birth to their second child just three months earlier. This birth came after several miscarriages. Three weeks before the shocking sudden passing of Phil's wife, his brother had died. This young man was caring for an eight-year old daughter and a newborn, and he had buried his brother and his wife in a three-week period.

I listened as Phil told me about his brother, his daughter, his baby, and his wife. When he finished pouring his heart out, he uttered the plaintive cry of the heartbroken: "I just don't know how I can go on."

I listened. Sometimes listening is the most crucial thing we can do to help someone who is suffering. In reaching out, Phil did the right thing, talking to someone who listened and understood.

Three Heavens

The Bible says, "In the beginning God created the heavens and the earth." (Genesis 1:1 NIV). Chapter two begins, "Thus the heavens and the earth were completed in all of their vast array" (NIV). In fact, the Bible talks about three heavens. We see the first one every day; it's our atmosphere. Birds fly in it. Sometimes we fly in it ourselves. Clouds float on the wind. The first heaven extends about seven miles up.

Any farther and we're entering the second heaven, our known universe and all the stars, planets, and galaxies in it. Scientists have gone to great lengths to discover its scope. There seems to be no end to it. But there is! God created a heaven beyond the second one.

The third heaven is where God himself abides. Psalm 33:13–14 tells us, "From heaven the LORD looks down and sees all mankind; from his dwelling place he watches all who live on earth" (NIV). Seated on his throne, God, through His presence, defines this heaven of heavens. This heaven is almost always the one the Bible refers to.

Together Phil and I concluded that, while the deaths of his loved ones seemed tragically premature, their arrival in heaven, where there is no pain and death, was a victory. I shared that since there is no time in heaven, it would mean his brother and wife were expecting him at the gates of heaven "now" in a heavenly sense. We discussed the disposition of unborn babies, because he and his wife had lost several.

I shared with Phil that my wife and I have also lost babies to miscarriage. I shared my belief that God would not keep humans who never sinned on earth out of heaven. We talked about how our God is a just and compassionate God Who is taking good care of them. And we will get to spend eternity with all our departed loved ones, even those who have yet to be born.

I believe that in heaven it's likely they will not appear as infants. Even in the beginning of human creation, we did not begin as babies. And since we were created for fellowship with God, in heaven there is no age since there is no birth and death.

I shared my vision with Phil that there will be a great reunion one day when his friends and family who had preceded him to heaven will greet him at the gates. And those who embrace Christ now and later will join him there when their earthly lives are concluded. Salvation and heaven mean we will never be separated again. There are no *goodbyes* in heaven, only *hellos*.

Sometimes it helps us to think of our departed loved ones as *arrived* loved ones, because they have arrived in heaven. Those who have passed might have left our homes, but they are *home*. Indeed, there is an African American tradition that refers to death as *homegoing*.

Phil talked about life for his two children here on earth. He knew that bringing up those two precious kids without a mom would be a significant challenge. There were church members, friends, and family who would need to pitch in and be there. In fact, regardless of how independent or self-reliant Phil might have been thus far, he was going to have to let people care for him and his family.

> *When we share with someone we trust, we no longer carry the burden alone.*

When we share with someone we trust, we no longer carry the burden alone. Phil showed incredible courage in opening up to me. I knew it wasn't easy. But his words—the stories he told of his loved ones—were a tribute to how much they meant to him, evidence that their earthly lives, while cut short, were not in vain. And the knowledge that they would one day be reunited was a great comfort to him. Their lives together weren't at an end. Far from it. Blessed assurance indeed.

Heavenly Truths

- The Bible has several different names for heaven: *City* is the most common name for heaven. But heaven is also referred to as *mount, paradise, better country, homeland,* and *place.*
- Heaven is mentioned in the Bible 550 times.
- Will they be happy to see you? 2 Peter 1:11: "You will receive a rich welcome into the eternal kingdom of our Lord and Savior Jesus Christ" (NIV).
- How long will heaven last? 1 John 2:17: "The world and its desires pass away, but whoever does the will of God lives forever" (NIV). Psalm 90:4: "You've got all the time in the world—whether a thousand years or a day, it's all the same to you" (MSG).
- What direction is heaven? Decidedly up! "Stephen . . . looked up to heaven and saw the glory of God, and Jesus standing at the right hand of God" (Acts 7:55 NIV).

The Bride of Christ

*J*esus never married. He proclaimed that the church, or body of Christ's followers, was to be his bride (Revelation 19:7). He did honor earthly marriage so much that his first recorded miracle was at a wedding in Cana. But his bride would be his devoted flock.

When there's a wedding at the church, it is a great cause for celebration. But the ceremony takes an entirely different tone if we rearrange the furniture a bit and, rather than a flower-covered arch for the bride and groom at the altar, we have a flower-covered casket. Revelation 21 deals with just this situation when in verse 2 it compares heaven to a bride beautifully dressed for her husband. As a husband I couldn't exaggerate my joy and anticipation of my marriage to my wife, Eva. But when we are confronted with our mortality, how do we respond if there is a casket instead of a wedding altar? Same church, vastly different outcomes.

I believe the Bible is saying we can be just as excited about the promise of heaven and the chance to be with God and Jesus for all eternity. The church is the bride of Christ—a marriage that has no equal and that will never grow stale. Now *that's* something to celebrate. Heaven isn't only a place. It's a transformation of life as we know it. A life without pain, without sorrow, without misery. A life with God!

He has seen to everything. The bridegroom awaits. Hallelujah!

Endnotes

[1]www.webmd.com/special-reports/grief-stages/20190711/the-grief-experience-survey-shows-its-complicated

[2]*On Death and Dying: What the Dying Have to Teach Doctors, Nurses, Clergy and Their Own Families*—August 12, 2014, by Elisabeth Kübler-Ross (Author)

[3]www.premierchristianity.com/Blog/Rick-Warren-My-son-s-suicide-and-God-s-garden-of-grace

[4]www.amazon.com/Path-Through-Suffering-Elisabeth-Elliot/dp/0800724984

PART 2

True Stories

Truly, truly, I say to you, whoever hears my word and believes him who sent me has eternal life. He does not come into judgment, but has passed from death to life.

—John 5:24 (ESV)

A Mended Heart

SUSAN M. WATKINS

Mom was serious about praying for her family. She dedicated herself to the task soon after she became a Christian. The first in our family to be baptized, she wanted us to be together in heaven. She fought long and hard, determined not to lose a single person on her "watch" to attain unilateral victory.

I've yet to meet someone as devoted to God as Mom was. Every outing and every errand were opportunities to share the Good News. When we went out to eat, she would still be talking to someone at the next table long after everyone else had finished eating. So she routinely took home to-go boxes.

She had a magnetic quality. Even when Mom tried to be inconspicuous, people approached. I had to schedule in extra time before and after all of her appointments to make sure she wouldn't be late to the next one on her schedule. Businesspersons, wait staff, children—Mom attracted everyone. She advised, encouraged, and prayed. For decades, I watched people come to listen to Mom talk about God because they sensed His presence in her life.

A cancer diagnosis later in life severely tested Mom's spiritual tenacity. It was invasive, and surgery was the only option to delay the inevitable.

After the operation, the oncologist explained the surgery and prognosis, telling me, "At the very best, your mom only has a maximum of three years to live."

Realizing that he didn't have the benefit of Mom's determined faith, I replied, "You don't know my mother. We'll see you in five years."

Five years later, we were back in the oncologist's office. He congratulated her on her unexpected fifth anniversary but

> *He bowed his head, and together they prayed for his salvation.*

delivered unwelcome news. Another very aggressive cancer was invading her body, and surgery was her only option, yet again.

During his post-op conversation, the doctor predicted anew that Mom only had a few years left to live, but after another five years and numerous tests, she was still alive.

At that subsequent visit to the oncologist, she asked: "Would you like to pray with me to receive Christ?"

In response, he bowed his head and together they prayed for his salvation.

Later, Mom shared with me that if she had never had cancer, she wouldn't have met the people who specialized in that field. Many came to Christ because of her, and she felt her surgeries and sacrifice were an insignificant exchange for their salvation.

Mom's Graduation to Heaven Nears

Ten years after the first diagnosis, Mom's final results came back miraculously negative. The cancer never returned, and her purposeful life continued another decade. When her health declined, I moved her into my home. She prayed to reach her eightieth birthday. Given her relationship with the Lord, I had no doubt she would reach that goal.

At the restaurant for her birthday celebration, she proudly informed everyone she met the reason she was there. People visited our table throughout the meal, wishing her well while telling her their deepest troubles.

But it was clear to me that her graduation to heaven wasn't far away. I couldn't fathom life without her, as she was my beacon in every storm. Within months, hospice nurses filled our home. I watched them enter her bedroom and then exit sobbing. They told me how she had comforted *them* when they were supposed to comfort her. I nodded knowingly. To the very last, she ministered to people.

Then Mom became comatose, and I asked the Lord to alert me before He took her. Suddenly, I knew it was time and rushed back into her room. There was a palpable change; His holiness and majesty engulfed the small space. Time seemed to stop, and I discovered a single tear resting on her cheek. I knew immediately she was beholding her Bridegroom.

The presence and power of the Lord was suddenly overwhelming. I struggled to remain upright, but my body gave way under the weight of His glory and presence. It felt as if the ceiling led to a direct pathway out of Earth's confines.

I gathered Mom in my arms and lovingly told her she could leave. I was reassured that we would be reunited eternally. Her heart leaped its last as her failing hand grasped her Creator's.

I felt the "portal" slowly close behind her. I was awash with grief, yet felt deep joy knowing she was with God.

In the following days, I leaned heavily upon the Lord. He is indeed near to the brokenhearted, and His comforting presence blesses those who mourn.

After Mom died, a devoted hospice nurse sent me a jack-in-the-pulpit plant in her honor. It was supposed to bloom only in early summer, but it sent up white flowers whenever my sorrow was at its greatest, despite the season, showcasing the Almighty's compassionate love.

> *It sent up white flowers whenever my grief was at its greatest.*

Some days my only prayers were tears, but thankfully God is fluent in that language, and He wiped them away. I had plenty of moments when I thought this anguish was my new normal. Mom had urged me not to grieve for long, but I also knew rushing the process or suppressing it would only make the pain resurface.

A few months afterward, I was having a particularly difficult day. I entered Mom's bedroom and collapsed on her bed crying. When I rolled onto my back and looked up, something caught my attention. Her ceiling fan had two pull chains with small bear ballerinas. Despite the room's stillness, both bears swayed ever so slightly, bringing comfort and reassurance that heaven had noticed my sadness.

Mom's Influence Lives On

Sometime later, I learned of a grief group and met a dozen elderly widows all mourning their husbands. It didn't seem like it was for me, but the Lord prodded me to return. I remembered how Mom had used every occasion to share God's love. So I continued going to meetings.

By the third week, the group was in tears, not from sorrow but laughter from stories of my mom. I'd become just like her—ministering to others instead of focusing on my sadness. To laugh in the midst of pain is a blessing and transports the brokenhearted to joyfulness.

The group was in tears, not from sorrow but laughter from stories of my mom.

I still feel Mom's presence whenever I find myself saying or doing something she did. I'm elated whenever it happens, honored that I am the apple that fell from her tree.

Though I still have my moments when a window of mourning opens unexpectedly, prayer helps. God even comforts me through dreams about my mom that frequently include her wisdom. The sorrow lifts and I often awaken from laughing with her while dreaming.

God is merciful to us and answers our prayers even before we express them. I trusted Him with my shattered pieces, and He tenderly mended my broken heart.

Belden Island Magic

DIANALEE VELIE

*B*elden Island is magical, ethereal, picturesque—like swimming at midnight under a full ivory moon with two white swans circling under the stars. A surreal portrait in black and white, a fantasy I could not have dreamed about but was blessed to live.

Belden Island is a small, rocky outcropping off the coast of Branford, Connecticut, a ten-minute boat ride from the mainland in the Thimble Islands. There is only one dwelling on the island, inhabited by one woman, my friend Chick. She lives there from May 1 to November 1, surrounded by gulls, herons, sun, peace, and solitude. Verandas surround her gray clapboard house, and there are no curtains on any windows. The sea and the house are one.

I have known Chick since birth; we are only nine months apart. My mother raised us together, rescuing Chick from the madness of an alcoholic mother who was institutionalized soon after Chick was born. Chick's father, our family friend and doctor, entrusted Chick into my mother's care, and we grew up more like siblings than close friends.

We stayed in touch throughout the years, and this May she repaid my mother's kindness by sheltering me for the summer. Having gone through her own wretched divorce from a doctor, she knew exactly what I was experiencing; I was wading through the same horrors.

At first, I thought spending so much time away from home would be an impossibility, but as the ferry shuttled me to the island for the first time, I fell in love with the sun, the sand, and the solitude. For the first few days, I sat on the beach and watched the rocks tumble obstinately into the sea, as jumbled, jagged, and disconnected as my own thoughts. Pages of unread poetry books lay next to me, flying open in the breeze. Waves crashed at my feet, numbing my mind and my senses. This would be my temporary haven, my retreat.

At night, the magic began. My mind, so numb during the day, awoke with the moon and danced. Tucked beneath a pink quilted blanket in the twin bed under the eaves, I felt like a caterpillar in a cocoon—an ancient phoenix, embryonic yet old, gathering the strength to slowly break out of its shell, controlling the urge to recoil, to never fly alone. I strolled in dreams where hidden memories and future fantasies collided. My fear-filled divorce nightmares ultimately stopped, and I began to constantly dream of my childhood sweetheart and first husband, Joe, who had died years ago. I kept my secret dreams to myself, sharing them faithfully every morning with only my pen and journal.

I was lulled into the rhythm of island life. There is no electricity on Belden, only gaslight and candles. I began to rise with the sunlight splashing into my window each morning and retire with the gentle ripple of moonlight each night. I wrote and read and looked forward to my dreams. The times I did leave the island to check my mail and pay bills left me edgy and anxious to go back.

Feeling Joe's Presence

My island rhythm was broken one Saturday when Chick decided to give a huge party. My sister was one of the first to arrive, along with Leona and Ronnie, friends of mine from high school, who had double-dated with Joe and me so many years ago. As we chopped and cooked, getting ready to greet each arriving ferry, we listened to a battery-operated radio playing oldies from the 1960s. My sister finally paused in her culinary musings and said, "I have this funny feeling. I feel like Joe Velie is going to just waltz in here and take you in his arms."

She did not know that in my dreams, he had been doing that every night on Belden Island. Her comment was quickly followed by Leona and Ronnie saying they were just talking about the same thing. They really felt his presence in the room, as if at any moment, we would all be going out to Babs and Bunny's, our old hangout, for pizza. I smiled, content with my dreams, and continued to chop.

> *I fell in love with the sun, the sand, and the solitude.*

We went out to greet the ferry and arriving guests. The wind was picking up and we laughed, little children once again, as a huge bouquet of helium-filled Happy Birthday balloons blew onto the island, becoming tangled in one of the pine trees. Ronnie climbed the tree, got them down, and tied them to the porch railing. Every arriving guest asked whose birthday it was, and we all retold the story. No one's birthday that we knew. Someone on the mainland, now without balloons.

The party was a huge success. People sat on the verandas enjoying spectacular views, swam, sunned, fished, or sailed. Suddenly, around four o'clock, the skies darkened in the west, and a storm brought the partiers scurrying onto the porches. We watched the torrential rain and lightning approach and then disappear as quickly as it had arrived.

As everyone ventured back outside, there were gasps of amazement. A double rainbow filled the sky. A playful God, smiling down at Belden, had bestowed a gift. Cameras clicked, necks craned, and everyone stood mesmerized. God had truly spoken.

I quietly went back into the house looking for my journal, only to realize I had left it in my car on the mainland that morning. I would have to record the event the next day.

Ronnie ran up to me. "Di, do you remember the last time we saw a double rainbow like this? It was in Aruba with Joe."

"I know. I know," I said, content with my memories.

Evening descended, leaving only those who were sleeping on Belden Island to play in the dark water under the full moon, amid the swans and glowing jellyfish—magical, mystical, mirror images of water and sky that seemed to accept our human intrusions. Eventually I went upstairs with my candlestick, anxious to be back in Joe's arms.

I took the boat across the next morning to retrieve my journal and pick up the Sunday papers. Opening my journal to record yesterday's events, I realized I had lost track of the days. One day on Belden Island seemed to quietly slip into another.

I thumbed back to my last entry and tried to recalculate the numbers. My spine tingled as I wrote the date on the page: August 16. The day before would have been Joe's fifty-fifth birthday. I could hear my mother-in-law's voice telling me he had been born at four o'clock in the afternoon, after a horrible thunderstorm.

I sailed back to Belden Island fully awake. My dream-like reverie had vanished. Never was my life so clear before me. I had shed the anxiety and terror that had stalked me before this summer. My sea of despair had parted.

I have not dreamed of Joe since that day, nor have I had nightmares about the disintegration of my second marriage. Somehow, Joe came to tell me: *Get on with your life. You can do it.*

Maybe it was the magic of moonlight swims. Maybe it was the rhythm of island life. But maybe, just maybe, God was truly on Belden Island that summer. Maybe somehow the harmonies of the universe did converge for me that day.

> *God was truly on Belden Island that summer.*

I sat on the seawall the morning after the party and watched the same rocks tumble into the sea, plunging into the depths under caressingly calm waters, and I knew this part of my life was over. I had faced the dark side of the moon and I emerged firmly believing in Belden Island magic, in God, and in myself.

Voice Mail from Heaven

TERRI WEBSTER

Death snatched Mom in the middle of the night. We received no call from the nursing home to tell us it was time. No goodbyes. I wasn't by her side, holding her hand and making sure she was ready to meet Jesus.

Our last meal together had been a few days before Thanksgiving—a celebratory luncheon the nursing home provided for residents and their families.

When I wheeled her back to her room, her lap held a plate of extra desserts for her to enjoy later. I helped her to bed, hugged her, and kissed her goodbye. "I'll see you in a few days," I said.

That was the last time I saw her. My brother called me in the wee hours of the morning to tell me she was gone. She was seventy-six. It wouldn't have mattered if she were ninety-six. It's never easy.

Thoughts plagued me. *Was she with Jesus? Was she happy? Did she die alone? What did she experience? Did she pass peacefully in her sleep?* To this day, I still wonder.

Daughter-guilt hung over me. I missed those days gone by when we had laughed and enjoyed each other's company; when I saw her being Nana to my kids; when I watched her play the piano skillfully and remembered the few duets we played together.

Grief is an odd thing to describe. It isn't something you can see or touch. It has to be experienced firsthand to understand.

I felt it in a space somewhere deep within, a place I'm sure God created specifically for sorrow and grief. We had already experienced a lot of healing regarding Mom. My two brothers and I were blessed with a doting mom when we were young. Growing up, I couldn't fathom anything happening to her. She was always there nurturing and caring . . . the strong one.

As I got into my early teens, though, her struggle with alcohol had escalated, along with an addiction to prescription pain pills.

> *She was always there nurturing and caring... the strong one.*

One night, she drove onto some railroad tracks, thinking it was a bridge until she saw the train coming. I remember when the phone call came and overhearing my dad talking to the police.

She escaped unharmed.

That was her bottom, her wake-up call. She went to Alcoholics Anonymous and discovered a new life in sobriety.

Unfortunately, our parents divorced during my senior year in high school. I watched Mom become independent. She found her humor and acted goofy just because it was fun.

After I became a mom myself, experienced divorce, and found my own independence, we had our struggles. As she aged, it became more difficult to break away from some of the codependency in our relationship.

Mom would call and leave long voice-mail messages on our answering machine. Sometimes the machine would stop while she was in mid-sentence and cut her off. She would instantly call back to finish her message.

The answering machine was on the kitchen counter, next to the wall phone. Whenever I came home and walked into the kitchen, the message light would be flashing, and I knew it was either a spam call or Mom.

Each time I pressed the play button, I would close my eyes and exhale, exasperated, while I listened to her complaints and seemingly urgent demands.

In her later years, she lived alone, an hour away from me. Her arthritis pain became intolerable, and she found a way to get multiple prescriptions for painkillers from doctors, which led to another addiction.

Before long, she was in a car wreck, causing her airbag to deploy and badly cracking her windshield. Mom's car was irreparable, but she escaped unharmed. Neighbors and friends began to bring her meals, sit with her, and drive her to doctor appointments and the grocery store.

She called 911 for everything. When we learned she was unresponsive or high as a kite, my brothers and I knew it was time to move her into assisted living.

We found a very nice house in a nice neighborhood close to me—an answer to prayer. But Mom didn't think so. She hated to have her meds regulated by someone else. Her struggle to adjust was real, as it was for my brothers and me . . . painfully real.

A year or so later, a stroke sent her to the hospital and then to a rehab facility attached to a nursing home. She never regained strength in her legs to walk and had other health problems that required around-the-clock care. She now had a room in the nursing home.

She still called every day, though, from a cell phone my brother gave her—sometimes several times a day. She left messages on my cell phone, my work phone, and my brothers' cell phones.

She called 911 from the nursing home so many times, we finally had to take the cell phone away. She could still use the phone at the nurses' station as often as she wanted. And we could call the nurses' station to check on her or talk to her.

When Mom died, her sweet memorial service brought assurance of her new reality in Jesus's presence. Her story of recovery played on the video at the funeral home. Words of encouragement from fellow recovering alcoholics assured me she was indeed in heaven. I learned that just because her salvation in Christ

> *"God, can You somehow let Mom know I'm thinking about her, and I miss her?"*

Jesus didn't look like mine, it didn't mean she wasn't with Him.

Memories of Mom Hit without Warning

As with anyone who loses a loved one, grief will creep up without warning. A trigger would interrupt a busy day, whether it came in the form of an elderly woman coming out of the drugstore or of random wildflowers I drove past on my way to work. My mom adored wildflowers.

One day, I pulled my car off the road, looked up at the sky, and tearfully prayed, "God, can You somehow please let Mom know I'm thinking about her, and I miss her?"

Months had passed since I had last heard her feeble voice. My unsettled grief couldn't be soothed. What I wouldn't give to hear her younger voice again, a voice I could hardly remember.

Not long afterward, I came home from a long day at work. I ate a light dinner, cleaned the kitchen, and got ready for bed. I turned out the bedroom light and snuggled in for the night. I drifted off. I never heard a phone ring. But suddenly I was awakened by Mom's crystal-clear voice leaving a message.

> *Was Mom talking to me from heaven?*

The voice I heard belonged to a younger version of Mom, a voice I had forgotten: "Hi, Terri. This is Mom. I'm calling to let you know I'm here. I am right here."

She sounded so strong and reassuring. *Wow, that's Mom,* I thought. *She's leaving me a message on the answering machine.* Then it struck me: *I don't have an answering machine anymore. I don't even have a landline.*

Fully awake now, my mind raced trying to make sense of it.

I couldn't determine if I had been asleep or awake when I heard her voice. Was it a dream? Was Mom talking to me from heaven? Did she somehow reach beyond the spiritual realm to talk to me?

And how did she know I needed to hear her reassuring voice?

God knew. And that was enough.

I didn't need an explanation. The voice was real, and my heavenly Father was at the heart of it. I felt God's assurance that Mom was indeed happy and I would someday see her again.

I haven't heard her voice again since that night. I still ask God to let Mom know I miss her and I'm thinking about her. But the overwhelming grief has passed, while the wonderful memories of her remain, and I know I'll see her again.

I'm thankful each day for the mom I had while growing up and for the memories I have of her now. And I'm very grateful she could call me from heaven to leave a voice message, letting me know she was there.

Unimagined Joy

BARBARA YOUREE

Even after death, my father sent me a gift. He could argue, debate, become upset—even angry—over difficult situations, misunderstandings, or unfairness, but I never knew him to hold a grudge. Forgiveness seemed innate to his character. I can't recall ever hearing someone attribute an unkind deed to him. He was a good man.

I often wondered if his early life reflected a different character. He dropped out of school at age twelve because—he claimed—he couldn't learn anything there. He left home and found his first job, bartending in Kansas City. Being very tall for his age, he could pass for eighteen.

Bored with that, he "rode the rails" to California, where he worked in logging and, on weekends, took bit parts in silent movies.

Moving on to Texas, he became a real cowboy and worked for a couple of people who owned a ranch. Having no relatives, the couple offered him their entire inheritance if he would stay with them the rest of their lives. No, he had other adventures to experience.

Eventually he returned home to northwest Arkansas and, at age forty, married the girl next door. These adventures became bedtime stories for my sisters and me. But I always suspected he left some parts out.

As we got older, he and Mother rarely made rules about what we should *not* do. Rather, my father modeled how a life should be lived.

As one example of his many life lessons, he often said he thought it wrong to go to church with extra room in the car.

Extra room? There were five of us in a small car!

We often picked up two children and sometimes an adult. I hated being all scrunched together like that, wrinkling my Sunday-best dress. Today I usually offer a ride to someone on my way to church. But I fall short of carrying out most of his modeled lessons.

> *My father became her loving caregiver.*

I do remember the two "don't do" rules. He adamantly forbade alcohol and playing cards, which meant gambling, I suppose. My guess is that in those adventurous days he became very familiar with both. But for as long as I knew him, he never indulged in either.

My sisters and I grew up, married, had children, and moved away to cities with better jobs. We all kept in touch with both parents and came for visits as often as we could.

When Mother suffered with Alzheimer's the last years of her life, my father became her willing and loving caregiver. After she passed away, we all three offered him a place in our homes, but he preferred to stay on the farm.

We set up a schedule for one of us to call him each day. Two neighbors, who lived close enough to see his house, kept an eye on him. Even after he turned ninety, he continued to drive and to do projects, including repairing the roof, as a neighbor reported.

One summer, we three sisters planned to visit him on Father's Day. Our children, all grown by then, couldn't join us. We had a great time together doing so many of the things we had done as children, including eating watermelon on the picnic table under the trees. Daddy cut the watermelon, as he always used to do, and we competed in spitting the seeds as far as possible.

Another ritual we repeated was gathering around the piano on Sunday afternoons. Mother would play the church hymns as all of us loudly sang. Later we learned that the neighbors would gather on their porches to listen.

With Mother gone now, one of my sisters played. Daddy's voice had always boomed. I noticed this time that he began with gusto, but gradually his voice began to drop. He seemed tired.

We had all planned to leave the same afternoon, but I decided to stay over another day so his house would not suddenly become so quiet again after a boisterous time together.

The next day, he perked up and decided to repair a window frame at his shop in the barn. After prying it off the house, he carried it over. I sat in a lawn chair in the yard with a book in my hand, but mostly I wanted to be sure Daddy could handle the task at ninety-two. After a while, hearing the hammering, I turned to my book.

A few minutes later, I heard groans. I looked up and saw him walking toward me across the large yard with one arm hanging limp. A stroke. With my help, he made it to the house, trying to talk but not making sense. I called for an ambulance and phoned my sisters when I arrived at the hospital. The three of us were at his bedside as he took his last breath.

Needless to say, we were devastated. He had been our anchor. That evening, we sat around his kitchen table. The loss seemed palpable.

"We are now the top generation," my older sister said.

"Who will pray for us now?" All my life I had always felt that every difficult situation would turn out all right because I knew Daddy prayed for us. Now he was gone.

"You are sitting in Daddy's chair, so you must say the prayer." My younger sister nodded to the oldest. She did as we held hands.

After the arrangements and funeral, with people standing up to tell what this good man had meant to them—many stories I had never heard—I headed home, tears occasionally blurring my vision.

A vivid dream came to me as a gift.

Weeks went by. I grieved. I wondered what afterlife could be like—or even if there really was one.

One night, a vivid dream, like nothing I had ever had before, came to me as a gift: each gleeful scene appeared, faded, and was immediately followed by another.

Once again, we five—all younger and vivacious—sat at a picnic table while Daddy cut the watermelon. We played croquet together, laughing; sat outside at night and watched the stars come out; chased lightning bugs; and gathered around the piano to sing as Mother played and Daddy sang with great gusto.

The sun burst out as we all ran around the yard together. Suddenly, Daddy jumped in the air with his hands held high. The others faded leaving just the two of us. He came to me and said, "I must go back." His blue eyes glowed.

"No, no, please don't go. Please stay," I pleaded, holding his hands.

"But I must. And your mother is there." He paused and looked down at me, his face shining with peaceful happiness. "It's unimagined joy!"

Joy. That is the gift of comfort Daddy left to me. Of course, I still miss him, but now I remember him with joy and have no question about the afterlife.

Make Sure They Know

SUE A. FAIRCHILD

Say goodbye to your grandmother."

I cringed at my aunt's command, yet shuffled to the bed to obey. Even as a relatively new Christian, I knew this goodbye was only temporary. Ever since Gram had been placed in this nursing home, buried beneath piles of warm blankets to ward off the chill, I knew her death was imminent.

I recalled only a little more than a month earlier when I had introduced her to my fiancé. She had not been feeling well, and I longed for her to know I had finally found someone with whom to share my life. Although her doctor had said her illness was merely a cold, it had turned out to be a recurrence of her lung cancer—which had quickly spread to other parts of her body. Now she lingered close to death and would not be able to attend my wedding.

I did not fear her death, even though I knew I would miss her terribly. Gram had a relationship with the Lord and followed Him her entire life. She would soon be with Him, in peace, healed, and restored.

I grasped Gram's hand and sat next to her frail, broken body. I struggled to speak to her, not needing any response. Gram had mumbled or not spoken at all in the last week to the repeated good-byes my aunt insisted we offer. The staff increased her morphine daily to keep up with the pain. Now the staggering amount flowing through her body had dulled her into a semicomatose state. She barely moved, hardly twitched . . . her body was so tired. I prayed for her to be released from this pain and to be with the Lord, healed and restored.

My cousins wept nearby, distraught at the prospect of losing their beloved matriarch. Although tears stung my own eyes, I felt God's peace, something my aunt and cousins did not understand because they had blocked out the Lord. Soon Gram would be with Him in heaven. Soon she would be reunited with my grandfather, who had died forty years earlier. Joy filled my heart as I thought about their reunion and about Gram having a brand-new body, without the ugly sting of cancer filling each pore.

> *Joy filled my heart as I thought about their reunion.*

"It's time, Gram," I whispered. Her eyelids fluttered, but she didn't respond.

My aunt commanded another cousin to say his goodbye, and I moved, relieved to leave the hot, stifling space. As I stepped from the room, the cool air of the hallway washed over me. I took a deep breath. My mom grabbed my hand and forced a smile. She and Gram were close—almost like best friends. Gram's passing would be hardest on Mom, even though she knew the same saving grace I did.

"I think it'll be soon," I said.

"Did you say goodbye?"

"Mom, you know I did, but we'll see her again. I have told her multiple times it was okay to leave. She doesn't seem to hear me. Besides, this goodbye is only temporary." I squeezed her hand and she nodded, blinking back more tears.

The next day, we repeated the process. The time was near, and the staff had instructed the family to stay close. Although I wanted to be there at the end, weariness had set in, and the long days spent in my grandmother's room had drained me. Once more, my aunt told me to say goodbye.

I sat in my usual spot next to the bed, and Mom joined me. We gently held Gram's hands—each so much like our own. After a few moments of silence, I said, "Gram, it's Sue. You know it's time to go. God is waiting for you. Grandpa is waiting. Don't you want to see him? Everything will be okay here. It's going to be so beautiful there. Don't you want to see those golden streets?"

I searched her face and stared at her closed eyes, hoping for a response, hoping the morphine hadn't muddled her mind so much that she'd forgotten the promises God provided. I watched her chest move up and down with each labored breath. "You need to let go now. There's nothing left in this life for you."

Longing for Gram to Know Heaven's Joy

Unlike my aunt and cousins, I knew that to be absent from this room would mean to be present with the Lord. I longed for my grandmother to have that joy after so much pain and sorrow.

My mother excused herself, overcome by the moment.

As I stared once more at my grandmother's closed eyes and sunken cheeks, she fidgeted, and I saw her mouth move. My heart leaped. Was this the moment? I leaned in, surprised that she was trying to speak. I had heard of others at the end of their lives speaking—sometimes seemingly to those on the other side. I longed to hear her voice once more, even if the words were not meant for me. I strained to block out the background noise. Her lips moved again as she repeated the words, struggled to make her voice heard.

With eyes still closed, she said, "Make sure . . . make sure they know."

> *With eyes still closed, she said, "Make sure they know."*

I waited a moment to be sure I had heard her right. She hadn't spoken coherently in days. Now, even after all she'd been through, her main concern seemed to be about her family who had no relationship with the Lord, the same ones who would have no joy at her passing, no peace. I realized she didn't feel like she could leave without making sure they knew.

I looked around the room, but no one else had heard her strained words. Everyone else remained internally focused— while Gram focused on their eternity. I had no idea what to say. I wasn't close to the cousins and didn't know how I could convince them. I kissed my grandmother's hand and tried to find words of comfort.

"He'll find them, Gram. I'll try to help. I . . . I'll try. It's okay." These past few weeks had reminded me how different these cousins and I were. Yet, weren't these the kind of people Christ instructed us to pursue? Could I have my grandmother's heart for these lost souls? Could I help, in some way, to bring them the saving knowledge of Christ?

I knew I would try. Because this moment was Christ in action. God, in this room, working to bring His light to those who would not see, working through the energy in a dying woman.

Saying Goodbye to Gram

Gram's chest continued to rise and fall. She said nothing else. I stood on shaky legs and walked away from the bedside as another cousin took my place.

I found my mother in the hallway and told her what had happened. We wept on each other's shoulders, not only for the loss of this beloved woman, but also for those family members who would not feel the comfort of Christ's peace when it was done.

Within minutes, Gram left this life and all its worries to be with the Father she so dearly loved. I felt she had passed her worry on to me so she could truly leave this world behind. I felt thankful my words had given enough comfort for her to let go.

I sat with my mother and wept. We would never hear her jokes or have lunch with her again; we would feel the loss. Yet I knew I would see her again. Her body had been healed; her struggles ended. As my aunt and cousins fell apart in my grandmother's room, I clung to my mother and my faith and felt peace. I would do my best to honor my grandmother's wishes. I would strive to make sure they knew His truth so they would have the same peace.

The Big Shine

DEBORAH MCCORMICK MAXEY

Your mother has had two severe seizures, and she's nonresponsive. You need to come to the hospital right away."

The 3:00 AM Sunday call startled me awake, and the fifteen-minute drive seemed to take an eternity. I prayed aloud the whole way. "Lord, You know how many times my mom asked me to promise her I would be there when it was her time. Please, God, help me keep that promise."

It was all I really asked. Just to be granted the ability to sit with her as her life slipped away.

The news when I arrived was grim.

"The seizures were severe. It is not likely she will ever be coherent again." Her favorite doctor, who just happened to be on duty, met me in the ICU. "It's miraculous that your mother lived through the last month. But I'm afraid it is extremely unlikely that she'll be coming back from this." He explained that the fifteen days she spent in ICU just weeks before, suffering with two strains of flu, pneumonia, a stroke, and various infections, had taken their toll. "The best we can offer is to keep her pain down and make sure she is comfortable."

While the news felt like a giant kick in the heart, it was not unexpected. The entire last year, I had wondered how much more my mother's poor body could withstand. Watching her gaunt, unmoving form in the ICU once again, I felt God's peace like a comforting mantle wrapping around me, assuring me that He was with her, that He would guide her peacefully to His home. I had arrived in time to sit with her and wait.

The vigil began. With calm resolve, I was filled with a strong sense of purpose and direction. From the very start, I knew that I could be there for her day and night no matter what or how long it might take. There was nowhere else on earth I would rather be.

> *There was nowhere else on earth I would rather be.*

Hospice care advised me to look for any signs that might signal distress and call for a nurse if I saw them. I watched for frowns, tossing about, jerking, changes in her breathing. And when I rang, just as they promised, nurses arrived quickly to administer medication to alleviate my mom's distress.

During the hours at her bedside, I shared with Mom what a great mother she had been, and I pointed out how she had equipped her daughters to be loving wives, parents, and faithful children of God. Although my sisters could not be with me, I spoke for us all. Some part of me believed she could hear and take it in, although she never responded.

"I See Heaven! It's So Beautiful."

Sunday turned to Monday and then slowly to Tuesday. Mom made no coherent sounds. There were three days and nights with my mom only occasionally calling my sisters' names and my answering. On

Wednesday morning, as I sat sipping coffee my husband brought me, my mother's eyes suddenly opened in surprise. Her mouth gaped in wonder as she looked toward the ceiling.

"Mom, what is it?" I asked.

"Oh, my goodness," she said. She raised her hands heavenward and said with a voice of breathless wonder, "I see heaven! It's so beautiful."

> *"I see heaven! It's so beautiful!"*

My husband and I were stunned into silence. Not only was she responsive, she was clearly verbalizing the first words she had said in days.

"It's so beautiful." She kept repeating, as her eyes searched the ceiling above her. She seemed to be talking aloud, unaware of us, transfixed by the vision.

"What do you see, Mom?" I asked.

"I see my mama and daddy." She smiled and nodded, as though she were greeting them. She called the names of her siblings who had died, and her face was lit up with a smile we had not seen in years.

My mother seemed transfixed. When I asked what she was seeing, she would reply without moving her gaze, each answer causing waves of joy. "I see your daddy. And I see Pop." Pop was my stepfather. "They are friends now," she said, smiling. They certainly never were friends in life.

When she closed her eyes, her smile remained, and she slept. I wondered if she would awaken and be able to see heaven again.

Knowing that the miracle my husband and I were witnessing was a gift—not just to Mom, but to all of her family—I called my sisters and all Mom's grandchildren so they could experience for themselves this extraordinary happening.

At times, it seemed she was communicating with those who had died. She was more a part of the heavenly family she saw in her vision than those in her hospital room. She was responding to them somehow with nods and smiles.

"What do you see now, Mom?"

"Pop wants me to come with him," she said. She pointed to a place in the ceiling as though he were right above my head.

Suddenly, she took in a breath, and her whole face lit up anew.

"What is it, Mom?"

"My dogs. All of my dogs. Oh, my goodness." Then another breath of delight. "And my horses. They are all there."

As she began to tire, my mom nodded off for a few moments.

When she awakened again, she looked up and we could tell by her radiant countenance that the vision was still there.

"It smells soooo good," she murmured. My mother had lost her sense of smell more than seven years before. As though she were recapturing all the wonder of that lost sense, she closed her eyes and breathed deeply.

Leaving for Heaven

When she reopened her eyes, they grew large with wonder and she drew in a deep breath of surprise.

"What do you see, Mom?"

"A big shine. A big, big shine." Mom's gaze never moved from the place in the ceiling where she saw the Big Shine. Enthralled, she watched.

"It's okay to go to the Big Shine, Mom. It's okay," we told her.

Her eyes barely moved.

"We love you. We are so glad you see heaven."

She shifted her gaze for a moment to those around us, but it was as though she were looking through us. Her mind and her heart were clearly with the images God had gifted to her. In the same voice one might use to say, "Well, my cab is here," Mom announced in our direction, "I see the Big Shine."

She looked back to the Big Shine, unblinking, nearly breathless.

"I have finally found peace," she said, and closed her eyes.

And then...she was silent.

Nights turned into days, and it was as though my mother never moved. Her body was there, but it felt as though she were gone.

> *I thanked God for His tender mercies to her as she crossed over.*

Then one morning, Mom's breathing became louder. I held her hand and for at least the hundredth time, I told her I was right there. I prayed over her. I thanked God for His tender mercies to her and to all of us as she crossed over to go home to Him.

Finally, she took her last breath and was at complete peace.

When I left the hospital, I stepped into bright sunshine.

I leaned back against the warmth of the brick walls, taking in their heat. Closing my eyes to the brilliance of the sun, I prayed the deepest prayer of gratitude I've ever known. I thanked God that He gave her that incredulous vision of heaven that all my family witnessed, shortening our grief and sealing our faith in a way we could never have imagined.

My heart was so filled with joy. Mom had graduated. She was home in His perfect love, with the Creator of the Universe, surrounded by the saints. She was united with the Savior of our souls, the author of peace. As surely as I stood in a little patch of His bright sunshine, my mom had reached the ultimate goal: The Big Shine.

Embracing the Unexplainable

NANCY HOAG

I used to declare that there was no way we could sense the presence of a loved one who had died. I also believed we couldn't simply "know" a thing we couldn't see, taste, smell, touch, or hear.

But that was before two experiences that changed forever how I look at death.

Betty was the one friend who had always been there for me. After going through a crippling divorce, I had stopped believing in a loving God. Then, by chance, I met Betty.

She would come to my house, dial my radio to a Christian station, and tell me (like a mother to her child), "Do *not* turn this off!" She read Scripture to me from her well-worn Bible, introduced to me other Spirit-filled women, and encouraged me to pursue and develop my music.

For years, I had been hearing melodies in my spirit, though I couldn't exactly call myself a songwriter or composer. With Betty's support and backing, I began writing down the music and lyrics that had been popping into my head. The words and melodies spoke to me, soothing and comforting me. My confidence grew.

Betty would arrive at my front door several times each week, pour herself a cup of tea, and sit quietly on my sofa while I played each new tune and told her how my music was changing my mind about God.

Betty not only inspired me to play my new music, but she visibly reminded me of God's love.

When she died, I was devastated. I felt alone all over again . . . until one rainy morning after I had poured myself a cup of tea and started playing the piano. Suddenly, I became aware of Betty's presence. No, I didn't see her, and I didn't even have the nerve to turn around to see if she was in "her place" on the sofa. But I knew and whispered, "I miss you."

I didn't see her, but I knew she was in "her place" on the sofa.

When I had finished playing, I realized I was again alone. But there was not an ounce of doubt in me: Betty had been there, and I had been blessed to feel again her acceptance, her encouragement, and even her joy.

A few years later, I was writing at my desk and watching three horses graze on the other side of our road. All of a sudden, I heard myself sing out, "Hi, Grandpa!" I froze. I couldn't type. I couldn't turn around. But I knew my grandpa, one of only a handful of people who had made me feel wholly loved as a child, was grinning as he entered my cozy home office.

As a sweet peace hugged me, I recalled how my grandfather had made me feel safe and even happy in my otherwise turbulent and frightening childhood. He was my first music teacher, showing me how to pound out chords on an upright piano while he accompanied me with his fiddle or guitar. I remembered it was important to him that I felt good about my music.

As I recalled those times with my grandfather, I knew that God wanted me to realize I wasn't alone. I hadn't seen him with my own eyes, nor had I heard his voice, but he was there. For only seconds, for only so long as I had the breath to say "Hi!"—and then he was gone.

Today, do I fully understand why or how such things happen? I do not. But I can't deny the fact that I did "know" Betty and Grandpa had visited with me.

I knew even without turning around to "see" them. I knew because God had filled me with a sense of His own presence, along with the knowledge that not only was I not alone but I also was— and would forever be—loved.

The Mockingbird's Song

PAM ZOLLMAN

My grandfather loved to sit on the front porch and imitate the mockingbirds that perched in the mimosa tree. No matter how complicated the song, Papa could copy it. It confused the mockingbirds, making them swoop around the front yard looking for the other bird. And that always made Papa laugh.

My sister, Colleen, and I had lived here with our grandparents ever since I was six. My grandmother was the disciplinarian, while Papa would give us anything we wanted.

One thing he couldn't give me, though, was the ability to whistle. Papa had tried hard to teach me, but even after all his attempts, I could never get my teeth and tongue and lips in the right position. Colleen, however, had learned quickly, joining Papa in whistling a variety of songs and birdcalls.

Years later, we were home from the University of Houston, where I was a senior and my sister was a sophomore. When my grandfather coughed, Grandma looked at him with concern. But Papa waved her off.

A while later, he coughed again, then cleared his throat. When Papa saw the look Grandma gave him, he leaned over and kissed the top of her head but promised he would see the doctor.

My sister and I returned to the university Sunday night, neither of us thinking any more about our weekend at home. We were involved with our sorority, with our boyfriends, and with my sister's plan to marry in June.

Grandma called us midweek with the distressing news that Papa had been hospitalized with pneumonia, and the three of us prayed for his healing.

When Colleen and I went to visit him, he seemed as chipper as ever. "I'll be out soon," Papa promised.

A few days later, the doctors gave us the good news that he could go home

> *The first song of a mockingbird came around midnight.*

the next morning. But that evening, Papa died suddenly of a heart attack. We were devastated. Colleen and Grandma wept, but I didn't. I was too angry at God for not answering my prayers, the doctors for giving us false hope, and Papa for dying.

"How could this happen?" I asked my grandmother. "The doctors were releasing him! How could he die when they said he was well enough to go home?"

"I don't know," she said, her eyes swollen from crying. "I just don't know."

My sister and I decided to stay with Grandma until Papa's funeral.

That first night after my grandfather died, I couldn't sleep. I tossed and turned on my old bed, staring up at the twelve-foot ceilings. It was hot in Houston, even at the end of April. All four windows in my old bedroom were open wide to let in a breeze.

The first song of a mockingbird came around midnight. The streetlight out front showed a solitary bird in the mimosa tree, singing a complicated bird tune. It reminded me of Papa and our fresh loss, and that upset me.

I hid my head under the pillow, closed the windows, and drew the curtains. I yelled at the bird to stop, even throwing my hairbrush at it, but nothing stopped the mockingbird. At dawn, it became quiet and flew away.

Grandma was too overcome with grief to make the funeral arrangements. Colleen put her wedding plans on hold because she couldn't deal with her upcoming wedding in light of Papa's funeral. So funeral arrangements became my job. I was still dry-eyed as I picked out the casket and the clothes Papa would wear.

Papa always wore a three-piece suit, tie, and hat, no matter what. It was what he had worn to the office, and retirement hadn't changed this habit. So I picked out his favorite suit and a tie my sister and I had given him for Christmas.

Lord, what's wrong with me? Why can't I cry?

When Grandma walked into her bedroom, I showed her the clothes I had selected for Papa. She put her arm around my shoulders and asked, "Are you okay, pumpkin?"

"No," I admitted, "I guess not. I didn't get much sleep last night because of that stupid bird. Did you hear him?"

"The mockingbird? Yes, I listened to it all night." She smiled, the first time since Papa died. "Did you like the birdsong?"

"No," I said. "Stupid bird has no respect for the dead."

She squeezed my shoulder. "It reminded me of Carl."

That night as I lay in bed, windows open, ceiling fan on high, I heard the mockingbird begin his midnight song. I thought of Papa's teasing whistle and how I'd never hear it again.

Lord, what's wrong with me? Why can't I cry? I miss Papa so much.

God didn't answer me that night, and the mockingbird sang until dawn. But I noticed that I didn't feel angry, just confused. I fell asleep as the song ended with the first hint of morning staining the sky pink.

"That bird sang all night again," I announced to my grandmother.

"I didn't hear it," Colleen said, then bit into her toast.

Grandma stirred her mug of coffee. "I did."

"Why does it do that?" I sat down at the table with them. "I thought birds only sang during the day."

"Mockingbirds often sing at night. You never noticed before?" Grandma blew on the hot liquid, and then took a sip.

I shook my head. "I guess not."

My sister agreed with me. "I never really paid attention."

"Sometimes they're defending their territory," Grandma said. "But I think this mockingbird is looking for a mate. He'll sing until he finds one."

Later that evening, I listened to the mockingbird sing his heart out. I wasn't angry or confused anymore but felt at peace. And I fell asleep before the bird finished his serenade at dawn.

The next day was Papa's funeral and a hard day for all of us. After the relatives left that night, I collapsed into bed, feeling sad and lonely. I found myself actually looking forward to the mockingbird's midnight song.

But when midnight came, the mockingbird did not. I looked outside at the mimosa tree, but no birds nestled among the feathery pink flowers. When the sun rose, I went to the window facing the front yard. I looked out once again at the empty mimosa tree and tears began to trickle down my cheeks. I put my head down and let the tears that had been trapped inside me flow.

God never answered my question of "why?" but He did give me comfort in the form of a mockingbird. It's an ongoing comfort, too. Now, whenever I hear a mockingbird's song, I think of my grandfather and smile.

A Letter to My Beloved in Heaven

PEGGY EASTMAN

Do you have to go?" I asked my husband, squeezing him more tightly in my arms as we stood at the door. Jim, a lawyer, was flying from our Maryland home to Maine to take care of some legal business. I hated to say goodbye to him, even for a short time. "I'll be back before you know it," he said, kissing me, his hazel eyes glinting. He was forty-six, strong and vigorous.

The doorbell rang the next morning at 8:00 AM. I wasn't expecting anyone and had no idea who it could be. I opened my door to find two police detectives holding up their badges, just as actors do on television dramas. In voices that sounded miles away, they told me my husband's "remains" were lying in the wreckage of a small commuter plane that had crashed in the Maine woods. There were no survivors. Remains? My husband, my beloved Jim? I had held him in my arms just the day before.

As I stood there, numbly trying to absorb what these men were telling me, I felt physically assaulted, as if the weight of a pile of rocks had descended on my chest. I could hardly breathe. I coughed, trying to dislodge the weight from my chest. We had been married for twenty-one years; our lives, needs, habits, and dreams for the future were entwined like the branches of a strong, flourishing grapevine. How could I live now? He was my life; we had no children. I was a widow at age forty-three.

My body and spirit rebelled at the brutality of this loss. In the months that followed, I was physically sick, unable to eat more than a few bites, unable to sleep. I cried often. Feeling like an emotional amputee, I dragged myself to church. This was the church where I had sung in the choir as a girl and had been confirmed, and where Jim's memorial service was held—a service I seemed to walk through in a daze.

My aunt had pressed a small green leather-covered New Testament into my hands shortly after Jim's memorial service. This small book, she told me, was sent to

> *I carried the little green New Testament with me everywhere.*

family members in times of sorrow and distress. When she put it into my hands, it was open and a squiggly pencil line had been put next to John 14:18 (KJV): "I will not leave you comfortless; I will come to you." I carried the little green New Testament with me everywhere I went. I read this scriptural passage from John over and over. What, exactly, did it mean? As a believing Christian, I did not doubt these words. But how did Jesus intend to comfort me?

I came to believe that I would find that out in church, God's house. The church became my spiritual refuge. In that stone building with its stained-glass windows, people reached out to me. They invited me to join a new bereavement support group that was being formed for church members who had lost loved ones. At first I hesitated, stuck in my pain and isolation. How could I cry in front of other people, all of whom had their own sorrows? How could I share the anguish in my heart?

My pastor urged me to go. Bereaved and fearful, I went, as much to please him as to help myself. But there, among others who had lost loved ones, I found people who seemed to know what the agony of loss felt like. The group became my new family; they understood.

I also found a compassionate group leader, Judy, a church member who donated eight weeks of her time to get us started in weekly meetings. She was gentle and nonjudgmental; she shared her own feelings of grief for her deceased father.

A Simple Suggestion

Not long after we started meeting, Judy made a simple suggestion that has had a profound impact on my life. She asked each of us to write a letter to our dead loved one. She said that sometimes, when people who love each other have no chance to say goodbye, writing down words in a letter can help to sort out turbulent feelings and become a source of comfort and peace.

I was skeptical; I felt a sense of dread. How should I begin my letter? Wouldn't trying to write it just magnify my pain and make me feel worse? Wouldn't it just make me relive the shock of seeing the two detectives at my front door and listening to the horror of their words? *What's the point, since Jim can't read it?* I thought. But three months after Jim's death I sat down at my desk with a pad of paper and a ballpoint pen. The pale light came anemically through the widows of my den, lighting the room only partially. It was quiet; there was the stillness of waiting. The paper looked very white and very blank. *Oh, Jim, you would have filled this room with the light of your smile, the smile that was my source of energy,* I thought.

I felt the tears coming, and rested my head on the desk. Then, not knowing what I was going to say, I lifted my head and began to write. The words flowed; I was astonished. It was almost as if

> What's the point, since Jim can't read it? *I thought.*

Someone stronger, someone from above, was guiding my hand. Here is what I wrote to my dead husband.

Dearest Jim,

You left me so suddenly I never had a chance to ask you how—if anything should happen—I would be able to go on without you. I never had a chance to hear what I think you would have said in your deep voice: "You can do it."

Can do is the phrase that best sums up the legacy you left me. Without that legacy, how could I possibly draw breath now? How could I close my eyes in sleep, rise in the morning? How could l force food into my mouth, swallow it, digest it? How, without your legacy, could I jog on the park paths we took together, serve a tennis ball without you as my doubles partner, smile for others? How could I answer questions about insurance policies and house renovation?

You prepared me for the worst I could imagine: life without you. You, who taught me to pitch my tent on a precipitous granite bluff in Wyoming's Wind River Mountains among sun-whitened elk bones. You, who taught me the value of tough love: love that demands the best a person has to offer others. You never let me give less than that, no matter what I did.

Do not worry about me, as I do not worry about you. I know where you are, and someday we will be reunited in heaven. At that time, I want you to be proud of me and my accomplishments here, even as I want my Savior to know I did not collapse in a heap of energy-sapping self-pity under the worst possible blow that could fall on me. I want you to be able to say, "Well done, Peggy."

Yours for eternity, Peggy

As I read over my letter to my husband, Jim, something inside me softened. I had dreaded writing this letter, but I had done it, pouring out my deepest feelings. In wonder I saw that I had written—with help from a divine Scribe—not a lamentation, but a song of praise and gratitude. The letter celebrated the many great gifts my husband had given me: strength, a sense of excellence, courage, the willingness to try new things. These were gifts I still had; no one could take them from me—ever. I felt privileged, humbled. How fortunate I had been; many people never experience a fraction of the joys we had shared together.

Somehow, as I poured out my heart on paper, the agonizing pain of my loss had dissipated. Writing the letter was a major turning point in my life as a widow. Grief, that self-centered thief, ceased to dominate my waking thoughts and actions. I began to turn

> *I had written a song of praise and gratitude.*

outward. After all, I was not the only one in our church bereavement group who had lost someone very dear. One member of our group had lost her fiancé at sea; they had never had a chance to share one day of married life. I'd had twenty-one years.

And so the letter I had so dreaded writing, picking up my pen in pain and sorrow, became a thanksgiving to God. I have read it over many, many times throughout the decades since Jim was killed. What I feel now is deep gratitude that comes from knowing how much I am loved.

God did not leave me comfortless; He came to me. He kept and will keep all His promises.

God's Sweet Assurance

PATRICIA L. STEBELTON

My fingers caressed the worn pages of my mom's red-covered Bible. Seeking comfort on this gloomy afternoon, I had taken it from the bookshelf and retreated to the bedroom. It was a rare time of total quiet, but the ten months following Mom's death had not brought the measure of peace I had been seeking. Wiping the tears from my cheek, I wondered if I would ever know the answer to my haunting question: *What had been on my mother's heart?* I had thought she was going to get better. I'd been stuck on those thoughts ever since her death. Even as her health declined, I'd told myself: *She's going to get better because I cannot imagine my life without her.*

The reality had hit me for the first time at the gravesite, after the funeral. Four months earlier, my fiancé, Dick, and I had purchased a small starter home scarcely a mile from Mom and David, my fourteen-year-old brother. We wanted to be close to them. I was barely twenty-one. The plan was for Dick and me to move into our new home after the wedding and be near enough to give daily support while my mother recuperated from a year-long battle with cancer . . . and life would resume as we knew it.

Only by forcing negative worries aside was I able to deal with her illness and the immediate pressures of planning our small wedding. I had not taken into consideration Mom's health needs, but now they naturally took center stage. I knew that after the wedding, Dick and I would not only begin our new life together, but my family would instantly be woven into our daily lives. Even through frustrating moments of wedding planning, I saw God's hand at work. Neighbors, friends, and family had been a source of encouragement. A family helper volunteered to care for Mom so we could go on a short honeymoon—something we hadn't dared hope for. And I was able to quit my job and have more time to be with Mom.

Her deepest concern was what would happen to David.

It was only after she died that I realized how many times my mom had tried to make me face the stark possibility that she might lose her battle. I had rejected each effort, telling myself she would conquer her disease. My mother was a strong, determined woman who had taken on the difficult job of raising two children with very little help.

Her deepest concern was what would happen to David. Mom insisted she would live long enough to raise David as she had raised me. But I also assured her that my husband and I would always be there for him.

Mom's countenance brightened . . . as if I'd lifted a heavy weight off her shoulders. There was new energy in her overall manner, and she became more emotionally involved in our wedding plans. Dick and I would sit on the side of her bed and share our far-reaching dreams. She would laugh with us and make suggestions. I told myself she must be feeling better. The three of us drew strength from one another, and I just knew that Mom was going to beat cancer, that our lives would soon be near perfect.

Mom's Health Worsens

A few days after Dick and I got back from our honeymoon, Mom's health deteriorated. Instead of moving into our little home a mile away, we stayed with Mom so I could be near her night and day. I often wondered if she had pushed all of her inner resources and remaining strength into fighting the weakness and pain until after the wedding. She wanted her children to be safe and cared for—*a mother's protective love.*

Weeks passed with no improvement. The doctor sent Mom back in the hospital. To everyone's surprise and joy, she perked up with the new medication. Once again, Dick, David, and I believed we had reason to hope for recovery. So, when I learned she wasn't eating well, I made sure I was present at mealtime, trying to ensure she had nourishment in her body to fight the enemy inside her. And while I still refused to believe the nagging doubt that she wouldn't get better, I could no longer deny the fact she wasn't gaining ground and she was very, very ill. I worried and prayed harder.

I began feeling fatigued, unable to face the food on her tray. I suspected I might have the flu, so I went to see the doctor. I was still in a state of shock when I returned to my mother's hospital bed after the visit and told her that she was going to be a grandmother. But she wasn't surprised: she had already diagnosed my symptoms and suspected my condition. Hugging and laughing, we talked of her early days of pregnancy and shared our thoughts, relating as two women. I was no longer the child. It was a special time as I saw my mother through fresh eyes, though it hurt me to see her wasting away. A week later, a late call from the hospital summoned us to her bedside, but she was gone before anyone arrived.

I couldn't call her back to this world. When I thought of my mother facing God and eternity without the certainty of Jesus, my insides went cold. Was she ready to meet Him? I wasn't sure. My heart ached with the question: Will I *ever* see her again?

According to God's Word, if you believed Jesus was Lord and called on His name to save you, you would spend eternity with God. I was eleven when I made that commitment. Why had I never asked my mother if she had made that commitment as well? I found myself searching my memory to claim some assurance.

> *Was she ready to meet Him? Will I ever see her again?*

I couldn't remember how old I was when Mom and I began praying together, before I had climbed the stairs to bed . . . or when I first noticed the Bible on her lamp table by her overstuffed chair.

As an adolescent, I remembered watching her read that red-covered Bible. I knew that knowing the truth but not acting upon it wasn't enough. Despite the hours we had spent together, I didn't know what was on her heart. Had I been afraid to ask her?

Knowing God's Comfort

Months passed and I dealt daily with my grief by summoning all the beautiful memories. They helped offset the moments when I was suddenly overwhelmed by tears. I was lonely and scared. I had so many questions about this precious baby growing within me. I yearned for my mom's presence. My young husband and I needed wisdom with my teenage brother who was also dealing with his grief in his own way. I called out to God in my need but felt little comfort.

I rejoiced at the birth of my beautiful baby girl but mourned that my mother wasn't there to celebrate with me. Those nagging questions about Mom's ultimate resting place wouldn't leave me. Would I ever have any assurance this side of eternity?

Now, this early summer afternoon, as my tiny daughter slept, I was feeling especially lonely. Looking at my mother's worn Bible, I'd discovered we shared the same habit of underlining verses we wanted to remember or found especially meaningful. I began an increasingly diligent search throughout the highlighted and underlined portions of scripture. I found insight through these verses, gaining a glimpse into her heart and deepest thoughts. It was as if I was having a Bible study with my mother, who was now on the other side of life's veil. I felt a closeness I feared I'd lost forever and gained new comfort, before drifting off from exhaustion.

This new assurance that I would see my mother in eternity was a gift from the Word of God. It lifted that heavy cloud of restless grief from my heart, replacing the uncertainly with a joyful expectancy of Christ's eternal life. My mother was indeed waiting for me.

The Little Night Visitor

BEVERLY HILL MCKINNEY

I had heard of others who had experienced a heavenly encounter, but I never expected such blessings to happen to me. But that was before my appendix burst.

The week had started like any other. However, on Tuesday, I felt sick. I thought it was a bad reaction to a recent flu shot, but as the day progressed, my right side began to throb. I spent that night tossing and turning, trying to relieve the pain in my side. By morning, I knew I needed to go the emergency room.

The ER doctor told me my symptoms seemed like appendicitis. He ordered a CT scan, which confirmed the worst. Soon I was headed to the operating room for surgery for a ruptured appendix.

Things moved quickly. When I awoke in recovery, I was told my appendix had been severely perforated and poison had spread to other parts of my body. The doctor assured me they had gotten all of the poison out of my system. However, I would be on strong antibiotics for a couple of weeks and might endure some unusual side effects.

One night during my stay, I saw myself lying on my hospital bed with a glass dome surrounding my body. The dome was covered by hundreds of Post-it® notes. Getting closer, I realized that the writing on the notes was the many prayers my friends and church family were saying for me. This calmed me and allowed me to get a good night's sleep. After four days in the hospital, I was allowed to go home but with warnings that I was to do nothing.

Since my bed at home was on the second floor, I had mentioned to my daughter-in-law that I would like to sleep on the couch in the living room for a few days until I could get up and around. When I arrived home, my daughter-in-law had prepared a lovely bed on the couch with flannel sheets and a soft down comforter. As friends and family came and went, bringing food and flowers, I felt surrounded by love, but still had difficulty with pain and uncertainty.

Because of stitches and the residue from pain medication and antibiotics, I had very restless nights. It seemed that each night was harder to get through than the previous one.

Will I ever be able to sleep through the night again? I wondered.

> *I was suddenly overwhelmed with a quiet peace.*

On one particularly difficult night, I was agitated. Moonlight streamed through the skylights above me and left a trail of light across the front room. My pain and unease grated on my nerves, leaving me restless and unable to sleep. As I snuggled into my warm down comforter and glanced at my feet, I couldn't believe who I thought I saw.

It was a small boy who looked familiar, maybe about ten or eleven. He appeared to be sleeping. He had beautiful blond hair and a shimmering white garment. His head was tilted, resting on his shoulder, and he appeared completely at rest.

I was suddenly overwhelmed with a quiet peace. I slept restfully for the first time in many days. My little night visitor had brought me peace.

This experience was special as I had lost a grandson shortly after his birth ten years before. My daughter had identical twin boys. One of the boys, James, had been born without parts of brain or skull and only lived eleven minutes. To our relief, his twin brother, Jacob, was healthy.

My daughter later told me she thought Jacob felt James's presence even as a baby. She stated that as she would hold Jacob, he would suddenly turn his head toward her favorite rocking chair and smile. It seemed he saw something that my daughter didn't. Could he have seen James?

It seemed he saw something my daughter didn't.

Jacob was now ten with blond hair and blue eyes. I suddenly realized that my little visitor looked much like Jacob. I felt like the Lord allowed me to have a special visit from my dear little James.

The next morning, I awoke rested. I wondered if I had really seen my other grandson. Putting aside my doubt, I realized that I could recall every detail of this small visitor. His little blond-haired head rested on his tiny shoulder, and the garment covering his small body shimmered. I could remember all this in vivid detail, and when I thought about his presence, once again my mind was filled with peace.

When I told others about my visions, they laughed and said the experiences were probably from the heavy medication I was taking. I knew they were wrong and felt I had been blessed with some special encounters from the Lord.

As I look back on this time, prayer and God's touch played an important part in my healing process. However, the point when I began to rest peacefully each night and to realize that the agitation I had experienced was gone was the night I had a visit from my little night visitor.

Her Presence in a Stranger

CINDY RICHARDSON

Being nine years apart in age didn't prevent my sister Kim and me from being close in heart. Her joyous smile, hope-filled plans, and positive thinking were inspiring. My sister was better than a best friend; our deep family roots continuously nurtured our friendship. We also connected through shared hobbies and interests, matching temperaments, and common goals. Others could tell we were sisters because of our similar voice quality, mannerisms, and distinctive laugh.

As the oldest of five siblings, Kim paved the way for me with high expectations and goal setting for education, professionalism, and service to others. I admired her sense of style and proudly wore her hand-me-downs, which I then passed on to others.

While not perfect, she became a perfect role model for me. As we celebrated our successes and prayed for each other's needs, our bond deepened to the point that I often felt I knew what she would say or think on a given topic.

I never realized how much her life had influenced mine until she was killed in an automobile accident. Her unconditional love, even when we disagreed, had inspired me to extend grace to others. I realized traumatic events had never diminished her spark of optimism. I had spent hours aching for her and crying with her when she was diagnosed with cancer and went through a bitter divorce in the very same year. Her hope-filled look into her future inspired me to hang on to hope when I learned our mother had Alzheimer's and my teenager was going to have a baby, and I started facing my own health issues.

Grief wears many faces. When Kim died, my face wore the face of hope because I could feel my sister's presence in my grief. With each hug of sympathy I received, I could hear her say "Feel the hug"—something she had said to me when, through sobs, I confided that her teenaged niece would make me a grandma.

I could feel my sister's presence in my grief.

When I spoke at her funeral, I felt Kim's presence as I looked out into the audience and saw one of my friends wearing one of her jackets. I sensed her love for her new husband of seven weeks when I thanked him for cherishing my sister, giving her love she had never known before. I knew she was there trying to comfort his children when I thanked them for welcoming her into their family, giving her the opportunity to be a mother for the first time—even for such a short time.

Years later, I still sense her presence in the smile of my oldest daughter and when I hear my laughter echo the sound of Kim's. I rejoice when my daughters make decisions reflecting the wisdom Kim shared about life's journey. Kim had a favorite saying: "The bend in the road isn't the end of the road, unless you refuse to take the turn."

I see her strength in my sisters as they navigate challenges along the bends of their own journeys. Families will naturally sense these things.

And I even felt Kim's presence in someone not related to me.

Praying for Danielle

My sister was an oncology nurse. She never shared the names or details of any patients she served—except one: a beautiful seventeen-year-old colon cancer survivor named Danielle. Kim told me about Danielle's story, displaying a calendar Danielle had modeled for to raise awareness and funds for colon cancer.

The thing I most remembered was Kim asking me to pray for Danielle. Their relationship deepened past patient and caregiver. Danielle gave Kim a crystal clock as a wedding present and was thrilled to attend the wedding. And Kim rejoiced in all God was doing in Danielle's life.

Five years after my sister's death, God inspired me to start writing. I attended a writers' conference in hopes of honing budding skills and found hope of a different kind. I connected with a young mom who was publishing a parenting book, and she asked me to be one of the guest bloggers for her website. Shortly after the conference, the author set up a Facebook page so her contributors could get acquainted.

As I read about each guest blogger and looked at the photos, my heart beat a little faster. One young contributor named Danielle was a colon cancer survivor from the area where my sister had lived and worked. Her story sounded so familiar. Could she be Kim's Danielle?

I sent her a private message. When I read her reply, tears filled my eyes, and through blurred vision I read her tribute to my sister on her own blog.

What are the odds of this connection? I was beyond grateful for God's sovereign grace to bring us together in this unusual way. We made a date to meet in person.

The forty-five-minute drive passed quickly as I rehearsed what I would say. How would I put into words the meaning and honor of meeting someone who had been so important in my sister's life?

I didn't have to worry; tears said enough for both of us.

Danielle recounted how Kim had held out hope for her. I cried because sitting across the table from me was someone who loved my sister for all the same reasons I did. I could sense my sister's presence as we shared our stories of hope and felt her pleasure that somehow, in this big world, we found each other. Surely, if heaven has a window, Kim was smiling at us.

> *She described my sister as a bright light, shining for her.*

I absorbed Danielle's words as she described my sister as a bright light shining for her throughout her cancer journey. Kim had located cancer-survivor college scholarships for Danielle, had given her wig brochures, and most importantly, helped her to remember she was beautiful despite the ravages of cancer. That had brought hope to Danielle's spirit.

Danielle told me the way Kim listened made her feel like updates to her life's story were part of a best seller. I felt as if I were reading a novel as our stories converged around Kim's impact in our lives. I sensed Kim's comfort.

It's hard to process death, especially when it comes unexpectedly. Why would God allow a tragic accident to claim the life of such a vibrant cancer survivor, newly married, with still so much love, inspiration, and hope to give her family, her patients, and the world?

Reading my new friend's blog post describing the way she felt about Kim helped me. I learned the last time Danielle and Kim had met at the cancer center, they had discussed God's purpose for their lives, including a reason for suffering. Kim inspired Danielle to see that telling her story gave Danielle and others the motivation and courage to face tomorrow. Danielle wrote, "I think I was part of Kim's purpose on earth. She helped me become who I am. I will forever carry her with me."

In meeting Danielle, this stranger-turned-friend, Kim's presence has stayed alive for me. Every time I look at Danielle or read her words, I sense my sister's joy, love, and hope radiating from her life.

Our presence doesn't end when our residence is no longer here. Our presence can be felt, seen, and embraced for eternity in the lives of those we touch.

The Twelve-Minute Delay

BOBBY BARBARA SMITH

The phone shook me from my sleep, and my heart leaped into my throat. Had I overslept?

I glanced at the alarm clock on the nightstand as I fumbled for my phone. The green numbers glowed 2:10 AM. My shift for taking care of my son didn't start until 4:00 AM.

My nephew and his sweet wife had graciously opened their home to me when we received the news that my forty-five-year-old son, Dave, had developed serious complications from his chemo treatments. I lived five hours away, so my nephew's kindness allowed me to spend precious time with Dave and help with his end-of-life care. His battle would soon be over.

The doctors had given Dave the unbelievable news that the super-strong doses of chemo had shrunk the cancer in his colon, but one of the tumors had broken loose, allowing colon contents to empty into his stomach. He called to share the news with me.

"Mom, I have gangrene. The doctors say if they operate today, I may live two or three more months. If they don't, then it will be just a week or two. They are waiting for my decision, but I wanted to talk to you first."

My heart had dropped as I tried to absorb the reality of his words. Dave had always sought my counsel throughout his life, but today he needed something I couldn't give him.

"Well, that's a lousy choice!"

The words flew from my mouth like venom; then I took a deep breath to calm my voice.

"Son, I can't make this decision for you. But you need time to make this decision."

My mind was racing, searching for something to help my son. I uttered a prayer for wisdom and a suggestion immediately came to mind. "What about that relief doctor who came in this week-end? You liked him; we all did. Call him and get his advice."

> *I heard the fear leave my son's voice.*

I whispered, *Thank You, God,* as I heard the fear leave my son's voice, and rushed to his bedside.

Dave called that relief doctor. I listened as he explained to Dave what those extra months would be like—both physically and financially—and then he spoke this truth: "I can't tell you what to do, but if you were my son, I would tell you to go home and enjoy what time you have left with your family." And then he prayed with us.

So Dave went home. Hospice came in three times a week, leaving the remaining care in our hands. As a family, we worked out a schedule to administer Dave's medicines and handle other needs. It was bittersweet, but that time was so precious, as I continued to stay with my nephew and his wife.

Now my heart dropped again with the ringing phone. My daughter-in-law's voice on the other end confirmed my fears.

"You had better come. Dave is fading." I was instantly awake.

"Okay, I'm on my way." I was just a five-minute drive away. Tears washed my face as I scurried into my clothes and ran a comb through my hair. I knew I had to collect myself as I sat on the edge of the bed and reached for my shoes. I wiped away the tears and took a deep breath.

I guess I'm ready. How does a mother ready herself for the death of her son? My mind was clear, but my hands were shaking. We had said our goodbyes earlier that afternoon. Still, I needed to be there for his final moments. As I started to rise, I felt an unexpected peace envelop me, and I sank back onto the bed. An inaudible voice spoke to my heart.

> *I searched for a logical explanation for this feeling of warmth wrapped around me.*

Rest. It will be okay. You must rest now.

I searched for a logical explanation for this feeling of warmth wrapped around me like a tender hug from a loved one. It felt wonderful, and I wanted to stay there forever!

My body and mind battled with the message pouring over me.

It will be okay. You can rest now.

"No! It won't be okay. I have to go to Dave. I have to be there. He needs me. I was there when he entered this world, and I will be there when he leaves!"

I tried to pull away from the warmth that cradled me. I felt gentle hands on my shoulders, gently pushing me down on the bed, and I succumbed to the voice.

I awoke with a start and grabbed my phone. It read 2:22 AM. I sprang to my feet and was out the door and on the road in moments. I had one thought: *Get to my son.*

At 2:26 AM, my phone rang.

"He's gone," my daughter-in-law cried.

"I'm here," I answered as I pulled into the driveway.

Why Had I Fallen Back Asleep?

During the next few days, I didn't have time to reflect on the strange happening that night, but when I got back home, the memory of the voice, the gentle hands on my shoulders, and the cocoon of warmth crept back into my mind.

I could find no earthly logical answer to explain the events of that night. As I analyzed the memory, I poured over every possibility. I wondered if it was a case of exhaustion. Had I fallen back to sleep and missed my son's passing? Could the voice and warmth all have been a dream? Those possibilities certainly made more sense than any other explanation. But what about those hands on my shoulders?

No! They were real! I was awake and I should have been frightened, but there was such a feeling of love surrounding me that I felt completely safe and protected.

I was puzzled as to how I could be wide awake one moment and then lulled back to sleep the next. As I examined the memory, a warm thought poured over me, much like the one that had lulled me to sleep that night. I recognized the feeling and surrendered to it.

You'd already said our goodbyes. There was nothing you could do. I wanted to spare you that pain.

Dave had spoken this truth to me before the morphine blocked his brain. I had asked for some time alone with him that day. We discussed death and life beyond as I tried to prepare him for what he was facing. It was much like the time I had tried to teach my boys to swim when I couldn't swim myself.

My heart faced the challenge once again that afternoon, as I told him what I had experienced watching my mom and baby sister pass.

I told him not to be afraid and shared how his aunt and grandma had spoken of seeing loved ones on the other side who were speaking to them and waiting to guide them home. I assured him that he would have an army of loved ones in heaven to help him make his transition.

"You won't be alone. You have so many there," I said.

It was his final gift to me this side of heaven.

We started listing them, and we laughed as he created a visual of them jockeying for the first position. Dave had always used humor to defuse tension, and even in the face of death, he was trying to lighten the mood.

We laughed, but then he grew sober.

"I didn't want you to have to go through this again, Mom. I'm so sorry." Tears ran down his face as he spoke.

"Oh, Dave! That what families do. You would do it for me." I cried and our tears blended as I kissed his cheek.

"Well, that was the plan," he choked back more tears, "but I guess God has another one." Neither of us could bear the pain any longer, so we returned to lighter topics.

We had said our earthly goodbyes. As I sat, enveloped in this warmth and love, I came to a full understanding of what had happened the night of my son's passing. Those gentle hands on my shoulders were Dave's. He had come to me, somewhere between earth and heaven, and wrapped me in his love. My son, who knew that I had looked death in the face far too often, came to me, comforting me, protecting me from the pain no mother should ever have to bear. It was his final gift to me this side of heaven. He gave me twelve minutes, just long enough for him to slip from my world and back into God's arms.

Fencerow Fragrance

KENNETH EIDSON

Growing up on a dairy farm included a lot of hard work and was a profession filled with pungent odors.

Every evening, after a long day in the barn, Dad would enter the house, smelling like a mixture of hay, manure, and sweat. Then he would walk through the kitchen and head straight to the shower before sitting down for dinner. The instant he opened the bathroom door and stepped into the hall, steam rolled toward the ceiling, and the spicy fragrance of his aftershave filled the air.

After dinner one evening, Dad leaned back in his chair and looked me square in the eyes. "Son, I think it's time to shelve the BB gun and start hunting with a shotgun."

My jaw dropped. I loved quail hunting with him, but I never dreamed he would allow me to use a real gun at twelve years old.

He pulled a 410-gauge shotgun from behind the dining room door and handed it to me. The cold metal fit in my hands perfectly. My chest swelled with pride as my father drilled me on the safety procedures. "Never point the gun at anyone. Keep the safety on until you're ready to shoot."

"Yes, sir." My insides shook with excitement. I could hardly wait for our next real hunting trip together.

When quail season opened, Dad called his bird dog, Judy, his favorite hunting companion. She ran to his side, wagging her tail.

She seemed more excited about going hunting than even I was. When he lowered the tailgate, she jumped in and ran into the dog-house Dad kept in the back of his truck.

As I watched my dad's compassion for his dog and his passion for hunting, my admiration for him grew even more. I observed the way he showered Judy with love and extended more love to me.

My new gun had a little weight to it, but not like Dad's 12-gauge shotgun. To my surprise, he carried the heavy firearm all day without setting it down. His strong persona always made me feel safe by his side.

Dad's strong persona always made me feel safe by his side.

We walked miles down the long fencerow through fields of overgrown grass and followed Judy while she searched for a covey of quail. Occasionally, I would catch a whiff of Dad's cologne, which was quickly swept away by the wind and replaced with the fresh smell of honeysuckle.

The moment his four-legged hunting partner found the birds, Judy froze in place, pointed with her head, and lifted her right paw off the ground. Dad stepped forward and flushed the bobwhites from their grassy hiding places. He raised his gun and pulled the trigger. Birds dropped from the sky, Judy fetched them, and Dad would put each one into the large pocket of his hunting jacket. They made a perfect team.

When we returned home, Dad opened his pocket and let me reach inside and pull out the feathery, fat birds. I listened and watched while he explained each step of the cleaning process. Once he had completed his part, he passed them on to my mom. She washed them and removed all the feathers, and then prepared dinner while Dad showered.

The familiar spicy aroma of Dad's aftershave quickly faded amid the delicious smell of fried birds. Having quail was a treat since we raised our own beef and ate steak or pot roast all the time.

Soaking Up Dad's Approval

After several more hunting trips together, Dad let me go by myself. I mimicked his actions. I cut through the woods and walked the fencerow. My pulse increased when Judy suddenly stopped and pointed to a covey of quail in a pile of briars in front of me. At that moment, I understood why Dad talked so much about her perfect pointing stance every time she found a covey of bobwhites.

I crept up on the quails' weedy cover just like I had seen Dad do and flushed them. I shot, and a bird fell to the ground. When I hollered "bird," Judy leaped forward and retrieved the feathered fowl. My insides did backflips. I could hardly wait to see my dad's face when I showed him what I'd accomplished.

Dad already smelled of aftershave when I arrived home late that evening. The sparkle in his eyes confirmed his approval. I explained all the details of where I jumped the covey in the woods and how Judy pointed and retrieved the birds.

"Well, what do you know," he chuckled. "Fine job."

We enjoyed hunting together for several years until Judy died. Dad couldn't bring himself to replace her. He put his gun down and ended his hunting days. He had taught me to love the sport, so each season, he encouraged me to pursue my love of the outdoors, but quail hunting wasn't much fun without him.

The days grew into years, and I graduated from high school and joined the navy. After I had served my country for four years and was honorably discharged, I bought two pointer pups, Maud and Lucille. I raised and trained them as I had observed my dad do with Judy. They became *my* hunting companions.

Even though Dad had sold the farm by this time and I had moved two hundred miles from home, I still made the trip back to my hometown and to the same old hunting ground with my pointers. After some coaxing, Dad gave in and joined me on one of those trips.

> *The familiar spicy fragrance of my dad's aftershave wafted in the air.*

Every now and then, depending on the direction of the wind, I caught a whiff of his cologne, the same fragrance he had worn all through my childhood. I often wondered if the cologne had anything to do with the success of our hunting trips, but I never asked.

His face lit up as he watched my dogs work the cover of the fencerow for the elusive bobwhites. He chuckled when they pointed, and I flushed them.

"You've trained them well," he said. He patted my shoulder.

"I learned by your example."

Not long after the excursion, I received the dreaded call that my dad had died. As I stood by his casket, memories of our hunting trips, his laughter, and the smell of his aftershave flooded back. But a sense of peace also washed over me. I was thankful for those days spent with him hunting along the fencerows on our farm in western Kentucky.

My two pointers, Lucille and Maude, were getting old. I knew they would soon be unable to hunt, so I decided to make one last trip to the old farm where Dad and I hunted together.

It was a cool, crisp November morning. The dogs ran free, searching for quail as I had trained them. The old path Dad and I once walked along the fencerow had disappeared beneath the over-growth of weeds. I trudged forward.

Suddenly, a strong fragrance hit my nostrils, making me stop in my tracks. I stiffened and looked around. The hair on the back of my neck bristled, and the dogs suddenly halted and looked back at me. Their nostrils pulsated as their noses lifted toward the sky, sniffing. They had caught the same scent I had, and it wasn't quail. The familiar spicy fragrance of my dad's aftershave wafted in the air.

I stood motionless, savoring the moment. The scent faded. I paced the fencerow sniffing, trying to relive what had just taken place, but the scent of Dad's aftershave was gone. Overwhelmed by the mysterious experience, I no longer desired to hunt.

The dogs followed me back to my truck and hopped inside when I opened the door. I patted their heads just as my dad had always done with Judy. What had happened out there along the fencerow at the edge of a field?

Embracing the experience, I rested my forehead against the steering wheel. I missed Dad more than ever. I longed to see his face and hear his voice. The only sense I could make of it all was that for a brief moment, heaven opened and allowed Dad to let me know he was still with me.

A Visit from Grandma

BARBARA GORDON

My friend Nancy and I were eating breakfast when the phone rang. I had spent the night at her house, a high school sleepover. I didn't think anything of it until Nancy's dad said, "It's for you. Your mom."

As I headed to the living room, my heart raced. It was the 1970s. My parents did not waste phone calls on frivolous matters.

In a faltering voice, Mom told me Granny had died in her sleep. My mother described going to tell Granny breakfast was ready, being unable to wake her, and then realizing she was not breathing. Mom said Granny looked truly peaceful. Her radio alarm had gone off as usual, filling the room with quiet hymns.

Granny had come to live with our family three months before I was born. She was my first babysitter, constant playmate, and number-one confidante. Dad and Mom worked outside the home, so during my preschool years, Granny and I spent our days gardening, playing, and taking long walks. We were rarely apart, and I even slept with her.

Later, when I started riding the big yellow school bus, Granny welcomed me home and made me snacks. She asked about my day and cheered me on. During summer evenings, we sat on the porch and counted fireflies. When winter drove us inside, she taught me to play checkers.

Granny also taught me to love Jesus. She spoke of Him as if He were her best friend. Long after I moved to my own bedroom, I remember waking in the night to hear Granny, standing in my doorway, whispering prayers over me. Our relationship remained powerful and emotionally deep. And now she was gone.

Spring arrived a month after Granny's death, but my soul still echoed winter. The sweet smell of lilacs did little to lift my mood. Mom and I planted the garden, but memories of Granny in her sunbonnet, bent over her worn hoe, dampened our enthusiasm.

The sweet smell of lilacs did little to lift my mood.

Summer came and then fall, and with them, the waves of grief continued to rise and fall. One day I awoke, and Granny's absence was not my first thought. I figured I might be getting better, but still, I rode an emotional roller coaster.

One cold, early December night, I pulled the quilt up to my chin, rolled to my side, and welcomed the even, slow, deep breathing I knew led to slumber. Next came the dream.

The scene unfolded like a one-act pantomime play. The setting was our kitchen and the time was the present, December 1970. Granny and my mom were the main characters. Supporting actors and actresses were aunts and uncles sitting around our gray chrome-and-Formica table. My role was as observer, a one-person audience.

Granny, in her homemade cotton print apron over her plain brown button-up dress, leaned on the side of the refrigerator. She stared at her feet as tears puddled on her dusty brown shoes.

Mom's eyes were red, and her face was puffy. She placed a gentle hand on Granny's arm. Her gesture said, *It's time to go.* Granny removed her apron, her signal that she was leaving. But then a peace came over her, as if she was going someplace special, wonderful. In my mind, I knew Granny would not be returning. And yet, I was happy for her. Wherever she was going I knew I wasn't to be afraid, that all would be well.

> *Granny removed her apron, her signal that she was leaving.*

My eyes flew open. I was wide awake, my heart pounding. I lay still, wondering whether I had experienced a dream or an actual incident. Even in that moment, I knew the images in my mind would forever impact my view of Granny's death.

Thank You for sixteen years to love my granny, became my prayer. *And thank You that she left our home to go to Your home.*

A Secret, a Song, and a Sign

ELSIE BOWMAN

God gave me three precious gifts related to my mother's death: before, during, and after her passing.

The first gift took place a month before she died, during a meal at a restaurant in St. Petersburg, Florida, my mother's favorite place to be taken for lunch.

In the middle of the meal, my mom, whose dementia-induced ramblings I strained to follow, suddenly looked straight at me and stated with perfect clarity: "You have lost two mothers and are about to lose another one."

Stunned, I dropped my fork and stammered, "What did you say?"

My mother frowned and muttered, "I just told you. You have lost two mothers and are about to lose another one."

Mom's announcement was not just remarkable for its sudden lucidity. She had no way of knowing that two very devout spiritual mothers of my church had just been killed in an accident while visiting another church member.

At first, I was dismayed and saddened by my mother's prediction of yet another loss. It was only later that I realized the kindness of my heavenly Father in allowing me to learn from my mother what only He knew. It was as if out of His wisdom and mercy He had shared a secret with me, to ease the coming grief.

That foreknowledge was important to me because I was only seven when my father died suddenly, the most traumatic event of my childhood. My grandmother's unexpected death when I was a young adult was almost as heartbreaking.

So, knowing how I needed closure with my mother, He graciously prepared me a few weeks ahead of her death.

> The "Ann" added a note of glamor to her life.

Although her real name was Sally Baird Howes, my mother called herself Sally Ann Howes, after the actress who starred in *My Fair Lady*. Somehow the "Ann" added a note of glamor to her life as a widow with five children, who worked odd jobs to make ends meet.

My mother did not resemble the moms of *Leave It to Beaver* or *Father Knows Best*. She didn't bake cookies and wasn't usually available to listen to a tale of woe or give me and my siblings an encouraging word when needed. I don't remember ever seeing her in an apron. The words on the greeting cards like kind, gentle, and patient fit her like a glove fit an octopus. Although my sister, brothers, and I knew she loved us and would go to bat for us, we felt her despondency as much as her affection.

Widowed at a young age, she remained depressed for many years, her unhappiness often manifesting as jealousy, bitterness, or a critical spirit toward her children and others. She explained our existence by saying, "Marrying and having children was expected of women in my generation."

We often felt more like burdens than blessings.

Knowing Jesus's Love

*E*ven after attending church for much of her adult life, my mother did not express the joy Jesus promised would follow believers. It was not until later in life that she found what she was looking for—a personal relationship with her Savior that gave her life meaning, purpose, and the peace that had eluded her for so long.

After her encounter with Christ, she began to study the Bible and to pray in a personal way, keeping a list of people to pray for by her bed. At the top of the list were her five children, my name first because I was her oldest. Not long after that, I surrendered my life to God and joined her in her devotion to our heavenly Father and His Son Jesus. Both of us prayed daily that my younger siblings would make the same commitment.

In her early seventies, although otherwise in good health, my mother began to show early signs of dementia, and by her mid-seventies she was in the intermediate stage. She had always taken pride in her intelligence and sharp wit. How painful it must have been to forget names, then events, and finally, basic life skills. Once a voracious reader, she lost all interest in books. An accomplished pianist, she forgot the rudimentary steps to playing. In time, she could no longer carry on a conversation or even finish sentences.

A week or two after our lunch together, my mother began to wander in her senior living center—alarming other residents—and we had to make the hard decision to put her in a nursing home. It was not what she wanted, but she preferred it to living with any of her children.

When we admitted her, she vowed, "I won't last here two weeks."

Within a week, she had a major stroke that left her comatose. I or one of my siblings stayed with her for the next week, providing whatever comfort we could, but she remained mostly unresponsive. Her efforts to speak and the fluttering of her hands reassured me that my being there mattered to her.

> *God gave me a second gift, a song from heaven itself.*

The following Sunday morning (her favorite day of the week and favorite time of day), God gave me my second gift, a song from heaven itself. I awakened that morning with a feeling of great warmth and joy, lovely images drifting in my mind. Almost immediately, a song poured from my lips. This simple refrain expressed my mother's hopes and the fulfillment of her greatest longings:

"My soul is set free to see all of the city. (She loved her upstairs apartment because of the view.) My soul is set free to bathe in healing streams. (She could never get enough of natural water.) My soul is set free to make beautiful music. (Music was her passion.) My soul is set free to follow my dreams. (She was creative and a visionary.)"

A verse that followed conveyed an end to the emotional pain she had suffered most of her life: "I have no more sadness. I have no more tears. Gone is my anger and all of my fears."

I rejoiced in the knowledge that my mother had ascended into heaven. The song could only have been written by her, and I will always be grateful that my heavenly Father allowed me to hear it.

Later, I confirmed with Mom's nursing home that she had, in fact, been pronounced dead a few minutes after six that morning. I kept the song tucked away in my memory for the next several months to reassure me of where my mother was and to soften my sadness.

The third gift was given two months after her death as a sign of God's love and hope for all of my mother's children and grandchildren. It happened when my sister, brothers, and I went to scatter Mom's ashes at Blue Springs in High Springs, Florida. We had already honored her with a traditional memorial service at her little Episcopal church. Friends from her church and her senior living community participated there with her, but we wanted a more personal gathering as a family.

The weekend we chose turned out to be rainy and cold by Florida standards. As my sister said, the weather was fitting, considering all the storms we had been through as a family. The borrowed tent I slept in leaked, so it made for a wet night, but at least we were together, sharing food and memories. At one point on Saturday, midafternoon, all five children and nine grandchildren were swimming or playing in the springs. The rain abated for the first time over the weekend, and the sun peered out from behind a billowy gray cloud.

Suddenly, one of the grandchildren pointed at the sky and shouted: "Look! What is that?"

Everyone looked up and saw a rainbow like we had never seen before. It was a complete arch, but on its side, horizontal to the horizon instead of vertical, so that both ends were clearly visible. We gazed at the sky, awestruck.

Another grandchild guessed, "It's Grandma Sally, smiling at us!"

We all agreed that it was a message from Mom, letting us know she was still one with us and that she loved seeing us together. We kept our eyes fixed on the colorful spectacle for several minutes until it disappeared.

What better way for God to show His great love and hope for us but through a rainbow? It was a sign to all of us that the storms of my mother's life were over, and she was in a place of glory and beauty. That memory also has been a treasure to hold onto in every season since, a reminder of the splendor and the magnificence of heaven that will never fade away.

> *What better way for God to show His great love and hope for us?*

Hope Rides on Eagles' Wings

YVONNE KAYS

Will I ever heal?

Gravel crunched under my shoes. Morning light filtered on the narrow trail winding along the banks of the river. Huge ponderosa pines with their red-sculptured bark loomed above me.

Honey, my young golden Lab, dashed ahead into a small grove of aspen trees. Yellow leaves drifting down only intensified my despondency. Everything seemed dead and dying, falling to the earth. As days grew shorter and darkness increased, my depression deepened.

This campground in the beautiful Oregon Cascades was one of my favorite places. The clear, sparkling headwaters of the Metolius River bubbled up out of the earth to form a surging stream. But today, as I trudged back toward my campsite, the birdsongs and the rustling of aspen leaves in the breeze failed to lift my spirits.

Grief covered my heart like a heavy blanket. In a season of sorrow lasting for four years, I had lost my husband, both my parents, a close cousin, an aunt, my dog named Yainix, and now B.J., one of my dearest friends. I struggled to rise above each loss, only to be knocked down by another wave of cascading pain.

My friend B.J. and her husband, Dale, had hosted a fall family campout here on the Metolius River for many years. When Dale lost his battle with cancer, B.J. and her daughter continued the tradition. And now . . . only a month ago, a car accident had snatched her away, too. Family and friends had returned to the Metolius today to remember them in this special place.

As I hiked along, memories of her flooded over me. B.J. had been a rock for me through the grief. Her door was always open—so many heart-to-heart talks over coffee at her kitchen table, moments of tears and laughter. For more than twenty years, she had been my confidante and spiritual mentor, my second mom.

> *She listened and imparted wisdom from her heart.*

B.J. taught me about giving the gift of presence, sharing some of the most difficult days of my life. When my stepson was killed in a car accident, she came. The day my husband died from a sudden heart attack, she met me in the waiting room of the hospital and wrapped her arms around me as we prayed over his body. She fought her own battle with grief and depression but always had encouraging words for others and me.

Caring and compassionate, she listened and gently imparted wisdom from her heart. I remembered her patience and kindness. At her funeral a month earlier, I had stood to testify how B.J. embodied love to me.

Later, at the reception, I was startled to see a picture of her I had never seen before. It had been taken in her early twenties and showed a slender young woman with shoulder-length light-brown hair and a radiant smile.

The picture triggered a memory that brought tears to my eyes.

The night she died, I had dreamed of a young woman who came through a doorway and stopped to smile at me. I hadn't recognized her. Now I knew who it was.

Young and beautiful on the other side, B.J. had come to say goodbye.

I whistled for Honey and snapped on her leash. Sitting down on a stump, I stroked her silky head and stared at the rushing river. The memory triggered thoughts of another comforting dream, one God had sent a year earlier.

Being There for Mom

The phone had jarred me awake. I picked it up to hear my sister-in-law's voice, strained and tense. "The hospital called. They said your mom is failing. We're in the car on our way to the hospital now. We'll call you as soon as we know more."

As she hung up, I had glanced at the clock. The luminous dial said 3:00 AM Oregon time. It was 5:00 AM for them in Texas.

As I squeezed my eyes shut, a kaleidoscope of scenes from Baylor Medical Center in Irving, Texas, had paraded through my mind. I had been with my eighty-six-year-old mother for more than a month, watching her struggle with heart and kidney problems before she stabilized enough to be moved to nursing care. I had only been home in Oregon for two weeks when I learned she had been transported back to the hospital, her heart racing again.

Mom was a fighter. During a horrible car accident two years earlier, she had been cut from her car by the Jaws of Life and wasn't expected to live. She had earned the title of "The Miracle Lady" at the Rio Concho Manor in San Angelo when she returned to her apartment in independent living. Then, the next year, she had fought back from a stroke, moving this time into an assisted-living setting. Would she rally again?

Lying there, waiting for the phone to ring, I prayed until I fell asleep.

In my dream, I was in the basement of a strange house, looking for a telephone. I spotted one on a table by a flight of white stairs and walked toward it. Suddenly, I heard a familiar voice coming from upstairs.

"Is that you, Mom?" I called out as I started up the steps.

Reaching the top, I turned to see a long hallway. Mom stood halfway down the hall under a light, smiling at me.

> *Mom stood halfway down the hall under a light, smiling at me.*

I gazed in amazement. She was young again—her hair dark, her skin smooth, an aura of light surrounding her. Exuding joy, she looked oh-so-beautiful in an elegant suit. We talked, but later I had no memory of our conversation.

"I Love You, Mom."

Suddenly, the phone jangled, and I jerked awake.

Oh no. They're calling to tell me Mom died.

But my brother Eddie's voice came over the line. "She has stabilized again. She's on oxygen but is alert and knows everyone. Do you want to talk to her?"

What should I say, Lord?

When Mom said hello, I said, "I love you, Mom. It sounds like you had a rough night."

She softly replied, "I'm having a good day."

I told her I would call again after church. When I did, my brother answered, "She is about the same. Do you want to talk to her again?"

I told her about the church service and that we were having a beautiful sunny day, a wonderful change from the rain so common in the Willamette Valley during February.

"I can see from my window that we are having a sunny day, too," she said.

An hour later, the next call was from my sister-in-law. "Still about the same, but now she seems to be having some breathing problems. I'm going home to get a bite to eat."

Tearfully, I took Honey with me as I trudged up the hill close to my home to get some fresh air and pray. Mount Hood gleamed in the sunlight as I gazed to the east.

My heart was torn. Should I go to Texas again? I wanted to be there with my mother, but I had already made two trips to Texas in the last two months. I cried out to God for wisdom.

As soon as I arrived home, I scheduled a night direct flight from Portland to Dallas.

When I called the hospital to tell them I was coming, my brother answered the phone. "Mom is dying," he said through tears. "But she still knows everyone. I'll hold the phone down so you can talk to her."

I took a deep breath before saying, "Mom, I love you. I'm coming, but don't wait. If you need to go, just go to Jesus, go to Jesus."

Mom died an hour and a half later. When I arrived in Texas at five the next morning, my niece told me that just before Mom took her last breath, she opened her eyes, looked at the family gathered around her and said very softly, "Love you all. Goodbye."

Dr. Norman Vincent Peale once wrote, "There are some great people who live so beautifully that they make contact with God here on Earth. Then when death comes, they merely step across."

That is what my mother did. She ran her race well, and now she had joy.

It had been my heart's desire to be there with her when she died. But in His mysterious way, God had given me a greater gift—seeing her young and beautiful, vibrantly alive on the other side.

Tears slipped down my checks. As I wiped my eyes, I glanced at my watch. It was almost time for the gathering for B.J. and Dale. I needed to get back to the campground.

"Come on, Honey. We've got to hustle."

When I arrived back in the campground, I put Honey into my motor home. I could see family and friends congregating by the river. As I got closer, I noticed a huge bouquet of flowers on a picnic table.

Hope eternal rode on eagles' wings.

A friend standing by the table explained. "Please choose one or two blossoms from the bouquet and take them down to the riverbank. Each person can say a few words of remembrance, and then cast the flowers into the river."

I chose two purple chrysanthemums and clasped them gently as I listened. People began to share what Dale and B.J. had meant to them. Flowers fluttered down into the rippling waters. I watched the current sweep them away.

Suddenly, a voice cried out, "Look up!"

I titled my head back to see two majestic bald eagles circling directly above us.

Joy fluttered across my heart.

God had sent a special sign, and to me, the meaning was clear: B.J. and Dale were together, and they were with us. A beautiful reminder that love never ends. Hope eternal rode on eagles' wings.

A week later, I received a thank-you card from B.J.'s daughter. "I was cleaning out some of Mom's things and thought you might like to have this."

A small flat stone with two tiny white flowers fell out of the envelope. I read the inscription and clutched the stone to my heart. *Turn it over to God*: B.J.'s final words to me. Then I took a deep breath and squared my shoulders.

God held me and my loved ones in His capable hands. My job was to press on with pluck, knowing He still had things for me to do here . . . good things.

And like the eagle, I would mount up on wings of faith, soaring toward the light.

Always with Me

MARK A. BRADY

In most homes where an older person lives, there is often a spot, sometimes in the TV room, where the eldest member of the family always sits. This was the case in the home where I grew up. For a while, it was the couch. You didn't dare sit or lie on it when Dad was home, because it was his spot. As time went on, Dad preferred a recliner. It didn't take him long to realize he could drop off to sleep as easily there as on the sofa.

Toward the end of his life, his spot became a soft, textured baby-blue recliner. The table next to him held his remotes—which he always got mixed up and then would wonder why the TV wasn't working right—a lamp, a magnifying glass, his Dallas Cowboys thermal cup, and his phone. "Baby Blue" lined up with the TV screen in perfect harmony. It was Dad's spot . . . his chair.

I was in Dad's house by myself several times after he passed away. Even though he was no longer there, I couldn't bring myself to sit in his chair. I'm not sure if it was out of respect or because he used hair products that stuck on the towel he kept on the headrest. Then, one day while I was there, I decided to throw away that towel.

We had decided to hold an estate sale after everyone got whatever reminders of Dad he or she wanted. No one took "Baby Blue." I'm not aware of their reasons, but I didn't particularly like recliners, either. And the color of the chair wouldn't go with the rest of the motif in my living room. But the main reason I didn't want the chair was that it reminded me too much of Dad.

We had shared too many conversations while he was sitting in his chair, his spot. Some I would rather not remember. Some got too loud, and too many hurtful words were spoken.

I loved my father very much. He was a very hard worker. He was amazingly friendly. It was as if he personally knew everyone shopping at Walmart on any given day and wanted to catch up with him or her. He could fix most things. He provided for the family's needs and was the greatest fisherman I have ever known. The last three times my father and I went fishing, we kept 167 of our catch.

> *I heard a voice say, "Go sit in your father's chair."*

The best thing, though, that my father did, along with my mother, was to take us to church faithfully. We seldom missed. In fact, some of my first memories are sitting on the back pew of a church. I heard the gospel and accepted Jesus Christ at a very young age.

So from my father I learned how to fish, spend time with people, and be generous. I learned to be a faithful, loyal, and hard worker. But putting his chair, his spot, in my house and perhaps making it my spot was not the way I wanted to remember him.

One day, while I was working at Dad's house and preparing for the estate sale, I heard a voice say, "Go sit in your father's chair."

I knew it was direction from God, but I wouldn't do it. "No, God. Sorry, but I don't want to." The thought of sitting in his spot was too much.

The last night I was in the house, I heard God once again tell me to sit in my father's chair. This time though, the message was a little louder and more forceful.

I went to the recliner, and sat in it. It felt as if Dad had sat in it for so many years that the chair had formed to his body.

> *I pray he will be a patriarch after God's own heart.*

I didn't know what to do next. I closed my eyes but knew I wouldn't fall asleep. Then I said to God, "Okay, God. I'm sitting in Dad's chair. I'm in his spot. Now what?"

After a few minutes, I heard the Spirit of God whisper, "Your father was the patriarch of this family. He ruled with unresolved hurt and pain in his own heart. But now you are to be the patriarch of the family, and you are to rule with love, forgiveness, and peace."

I sat there and cried. My family did need a lot of healing, a lot of prayer, and a lot of love. I accepted God's decree, but I knew I would need His help, patience, power, and might to be the type of loving, understanding patriarch He desired.

A patriarch is the oldest member of a group, but he is also a person who is the founder of something. I preferred the second definition. I wanted to start a new way for my family members to love, speak, and react to one another. I wanted them to show respect.

As I sat in my father's chair, I was comforted in the loss of my father. Perhaps what God had shared with me were the same goals He had set out for my father as well. These were good goals for any family to have, and now my family would have an opportunity to live them.

We did have the estate sale, but no one bought "Baby Blue." I laughed as I told God, "No, I'm still not taking this chair and putting it in my house."

I moved it into the garage, and it sat there for a few days until I convinced a young man to take it for free. I persuaded him to take the chair by bragging on its color, and showing off its functionality. I told him it would feel good to come home from a long day's work and relax in his new chair, and that all would soon know it was his chair, his spot. I pray the young man will be a patriarch after God's own heart for his family.

"Baby Blue" may be gone, but I will always have the memories of my father sitting in his chair, in his spot. *Love ya, Dad, and thank You, God, for using Dad's chair to speak to my heart and direct my steps. I love You, too, God, and know this, Your spot will forever be in my heart.*

A Fluffy Messenger

ELIZABETH GARRETT

When my husband, Phillip, kissed me goodbye that crisp September morning, I felt uneasy.

Instead of the usual quick kiss and "I love you, little rabbit," he cupped my face in his hands and gave me a lingering kiss. No "little rabbit," no smile, just a blank, solemn gaze.

When he used my pet name, I knew he was his usual playful self, but he hadn't said it in weeks.

Since moving to care for my elderly mother, we had made numerous changes, including health care providers. The new doctor prescribed Phillip a different blood pressure medication. I didn't pay attention to the black box warning about potential suicidal thoughts. During the first two months of taking it, I noticed physical side effects, but Phillip felt like he could live with them.

When the doctor added a medication for high cholesterol prevention ten weeks later, I immediately noticed a change in Phillip's mental disposition. While home, he stopped wanting to ride around the property in the golf cart. All he felt like doing was sleeping, although he had worked nonstop in the past. When we were with friends and family, he never seemed engaged, like he was just going through the motions.

We had taken on new debt, and home-building plans had been delayed. When I approached the subject of his being "in a funk" earlier that week, Phillip made me believe he would feel better about things after we moved into our new home.

After the cherished kiss, I sensed an eagerness to get an earlier start than usual as he hopped into his truck. I had scheduled us to go out of town to a friend's funeral that evening, so I figured he wanted to get to work early since he was planning to leave about an hour before closing.

Instead of the usual cheerful sendoff that day, deep down I wanted to scream, "Just stay home from work today."

Thirty minutes after he left, another nagging sensation pulled at my heart. I looked at my phone locator app, and he registered as being in a wooded area about seven miles from our property, right off the highway. I had noticed he had been there in the previous weeks, but did not understand why. He had mentioned his location signal must not be working, so I took him at his word.

> *Deep down, I wanted to scream, "Just stay home from work today."*

I put aside my fears and tackled the day's to-do list. Phillip had planned on being home around 3:30, and we would leave the house around 4 o'clock. I dressed for the funeral and did a few small projects as I waited for his arrival. When I checked the phone app again, the signal was at that same spot he had been early in the morning, an abandoned wooded area.

It didn't make sense. I tried calling him, with no answer. I reminded myself that his location signal most likely wasn't working. Still, I began making phone calls to his coworkers, and discovered he had left work earlier than expected, announcing he needed to take care of some business before going to a funeral.

The Search Begins

An uncomfortable feeling swept over me. I called family members, messaged folks, and posted on social media, where I asked for urgent prayer. After exhausting those resources, I drove to the area next to where his phone showed he was. Still, no answers. The signal came from a wooded area off the road, but I didn't see his large bright-red pickup truck. I felt confident I could have seen it from hundreds of feet away, even with leaves on the trees.

> *It seemed Phillip had vanished without a trace.*

The muddy path leading into the woods looked treacherous, especially for a middle-aged woman to drive down by herself in the middle of nowhere. Besides, daylight was fading, and getting stuck on a lonely country road didn't sound like a good idea. I felt as if God put His big, gentle hands on my shoulders and said, "Don't you dare go down that path."

But I was scared. It seemed Phillip had vanished without a trace. I headed back to the house, unsure of what to do next. Several groups of friends traveled to the general area, searchlights in tow. They, too, came up short.

Finally, around eight that evening, a retired pastor friend, Danny, stopped by and announced that God had sent him to help me find Phillip. He insisted we take my phone and drive to the spot where Phillip's phone signal registered. Unable to feel emotions and with no other options, I complied. We got in his truck and headed out. Despite the mud, we drove up the incline into the woods and down a small hill into an open area. I looked up in disbelief at Phillip's truck, complete with his vanity plate displaying the phrase CABNET1. An eerie silence and darkness engulfed us.

My friend directed me to stay in his vehicle. He went to Phillip's truck cab, where his phone, keys, and wallet lay on the seat. Danny came back to where I was and told me things didn't seem good, that he was going to look for Phillip. Minutes later, I heard loud sobbing. At first, I thought Danny had found Phillip alive, and he was crying in agony. Instead, Danny was crying since he had found Phillip's lifeless body.

"Elizabeth, call 911," he shouted.

Law enforcement arrived soon after the call. I sat frozen in Danny's vehicle while officials took care of business. The following hours and days became a blur. I felt like someone had pulled the rug from underneath my feet, and it had tossed me miles up into the air. Lots of objects were flying by, but I couldn't identify them.

Thousands of people responded in disbelief at the news of Phillip's suicide. They had never seen any signs of depression or anxiety. How could such a strong, solid man of God have even considered taking his own life?

The day after the trauma occurred, my friend Suzy traveled from out of state to comfort me. While I responded to messages, phone calls, and visitors, Suzy did some research, discovering that Phillip's new medications and their combination had incited suicide in many others. The more research she did, the more I realized his strange behavior was caused by side effects from both medications and their interaction with each other. I had an answer but no financial resources, an uncompleted house, and no husband.

An Unexpected Visitor

The first week after the memorial service, Suzy surprised me with a special delivery from Amazon every day. Each gift box bore a bunny rabbit with a special note reminding me Phillip was with God in heaven, and he would always be with me in my heart. I treasured each one and held them tight as if the inanimate bundles of fake fur could miraculously transform into my sweetheart.

Weeks later, my friend Tammy and I sat on wooden benches lining my mom's front porch. The benches showed no mercy to our rear ends, just like our current situation . . . hard. We gazed out over the rolling green fields as tears ran down our faces.

> "Oh, my goodness, Tammy!" I screamed. "Did you see that?"

Tammy had lived with me and Phillip for a short while when she was going through a tough time. He had become a father figure to her. Now she sacrificed her time each weekend to travel hours away to spend time with me.

"I just can't wrap my mind around this entire situation," I told her. "This isn't right. I feel so alone now."

Her temple creased, Tammy drew a deep puff from her cigarette, a habit she picked back up after the tragedy. She shook her head. "It's not right, Elizabeth. This should have never happened. We all knew he wasn't acting like himself, but none of us realized his agony."

Even my dog, Harley, seemed lost. He sprawled across my lap while I held him tight.

Sighing, I glanced at Tammy. "I sure miss that crazy ol' boy," I said as I wiped tears from my eyes.

Before she could respond, a bunny rabbit darted across the yard. It was as if it had come from out of nowhere and ran from in front of my mom's house to mine, which was being built hundreds of feet away.

"Oh, my goodness, Tammy! Oh, my goodness," I screamed. "Did you see that?"

"It was a rabbit! Elizabeth, it was running. Fast!" Tammy said.

"Yes, it was!" I said.

We both doubled over with laughter, followed by more tears, and then more laughter. It was as if an angel had been standing there telling the rabbit at exactly which second it needed to run. I imagined Phillip and Jesus "high-fiving" each other and bearing ear-to-ear smiles as they witnessed our excitement from heaven's vantage point.

I knew without a doubt what appeared to be a random act of nature was no coincidence. God wanted me to know Phillip was free and running at record speed . . . no more suffering from medication side effects or even a need to take medications. He was in paradise with his heavenly father.

A quiet peace settled over my spirit, as God had confirmed his involvement in my life. He assured me that my loved one lived on, just in another form, and would always be with me in my heart, just like Suzy said he would.

As I look around my now completed home and see my massive collection of stuffed rabbits, I smile at how simple gestures of dear friends can make a real difference in working through life's struggles.

While the journey has been a staggering, gut-wrenching climb, I know God is by my side directing every step. Now and then, He sends a cute little bunny rabbit with a white fluffy tail to wiggle and wink at me . . . when I need it most.

The Woman on the Bicycle

ANGELA JOSEPH

Traveling has always been one of my favorite pastimes, and I dreamed of one day enhancing my travel experience by going on a cruise. When my pastor announced that he was organizing a Caribbean cruise, I was one of the first to sign up. We would visit places I had never seen—Antigua, Barbados, Tortola, and St. Lucia.

We set sail from Miami, and the cruise proved to be everything I had hoped it would be. The food, the ambience, the entertainment, even the weather all seemed to cooperate to make our vacation as enjoyable as possible.

Now here we were, about to visit our last destination, St. Lucia. I was eager to see this popular island, especially its most famous landmark, the Pitons, two majestic mountain peaks rising out of the sea. But as we boarded the bus, my enthusiasm suddenly left me, and I stared at the passing scenery with little interest. The Pitons proved to be a stunning site, but while the other passengers chattered and took pictures, I experienced a sudden wave of unexplainable sadness.

By the time we got to our next stop—a rain forest—I felt sick. I assumed it was motion sickness, since the road was hilly and winding. I stayed on the bus and felt better on the ride back to the cruise ship.

That night, as I lay on my bed, for some reason, my mind rested on my family and to the baby my daughter-in-law had miscarried many years earlier. I remembered how heartbroken I had been and how much I had cried. I hadn't thought about the baby much after that, especially since Lisa became pregnant a few months later and gave birth to twins.

So, why was I thinking about that other baby now? I consoled myself with the thought that when I get to heaven, I would see my little granddaughter.

Then I had a strange dream. I saw a figure dressed in white, riding a bicycle. The person appeared to be a woman, but I couldn't see her face. All around her was darkness, and there were no houses or gardens . . . just this woman in white on a bicycle.

> *I saw a figure dressed in white, riding a bicycle.*

The following day, we encountered rough seas as we started to sail for home. Waves were almost up to our little porthole window, and the boat rocked crazily. Strangely enough, I didn't become seasick, but a heaviness enveloped me. My mind kept reflecting on the dream of the night before and the lost baby. When I joined the conversation at dinner, I forced myself to be cheerful.

Later, as my friend and I packed for our departure, the heaviness returned. I sensed in my spirit something unexpected, something difficult, was ahead. If only I could stay on the ship and avoid whatever it was that awaited me at home. As I looked through the porthole window at the dark and ominous waves, I silently prayed for our safety.

Dreading Going Home

The next morning after breakfast, while we waited to disembark the ship, the sinking feeling returned, heavier than ever. I've always loved traveling, but when the vacation ended, I was always eager to go home, see my family, give them their gifts, and tell them about the trip. This time was different.

When I told my friends how I felt, they laughed and one said, "Maybe the cruise should have been longer."

She was the woman on the bicycle.

I shrugged and turned to look at the Miami shoreline. Instead of welcoming, it seemed dark and menacing. I prayed that God would give me the strength to face whatever awaited me. As we disembarked and got on the bus, some of the heaviness lifted.

About an hour later, my daughter Karen and her family stopped over. My daughter, son-in-law, and grandson greeted me warmly, but my daughter seemed off. Perhaps she was tired.

I had managed to shake off the heaviness as I told her all about the cruise.

Then my daughter said to me, "Mummy, we have to talk."

I looked at my son-in-law. His eyes seemed glassy, and Karen's stricken expression made my heartbeat quicken. Something terrible had happened!

"Did somebody die?" I asked.

She nodded gravely.

"Lisa," she replied.

We never knew that my daughter-in-law Lisa, the love of my son Kevin's life and the mother of their three young children, was ill. She was so beautiful, kind, and brilliant. *She* was the woman on the bicycle. Perhaps when I had thought about meeting the baby she miscarried, Lisa was meeting her at that very moment.

"What happened?" I asked.

Karen told me that Lisa was leaving the house with her kids when she collapsed. She was dead by the time the ambulance arrived. She had a cardiac arrest. I believe it happened while I was in St. Lucia, experiencing the nausea and feeling of heaviness.

Disbelief, grief, and sorrow washed over me. Why would God take a young, beautiful woman away from her family and her community? Then tears came to everyone's eyes—Karen, her husband, my grandson, and I wept as we tried to console one another.

Lisa had been a devout Christian. When she was a young woman at college, she had joined Campus Crusade for Christ. She and Kevin were active members of their church. When I talked with Kevin, he told me that the night before she died, she had prayed with one of her friends whom she had been counseling.

Days later, Kevin found her diary, in which she wrote, "At the end of this phase, I want to hear Jesus say, 'Well done, thou good and faithful servant. You have picked up your cross, you abided in Me, you loved Me with all your heart, and you loved others and loved yourself.'"

I believe sometimes dreams and visions are God's messages from heaven to alert us to what is about to happen in the natural realm. When I think of the life Lisa lived and what she wrote in her diary, I'm convinced she is in heaven. The fact that I will see her, my granddaughter, and all my loved ones who have gone on before gives me great comfort.

Don't Worry about Me

KATHRYN GARDNER

The phone beside my bed rang around 1:00 AM, but, comfy in
bed, I just ignored it. It rang again some time later. I didn't even
turn over. I had been out late on a singing gig and didn't want to be
bothered. Never did I think the call could be a life-or-death matter.

When finally I woke up, I listened to a voice mail telling me
my eighty-five-year-old mother had fallen and was being taken by
ambulance to a nearby hospital. My cousins, who lived across the
street, had been there for her, but neither my brother nor I had been.

The doctors confirmed she had broken her hip and that it would
need to be replaced. I insisted she be transferred to a hospital in
Memphis, where her regular cardiologist and internist could see her.

I met her there. Considering what she had been through, she
looked amazing to me. Still I felt guilty that I hadn't answered the
phone and been able to respond more quickly.

The nurse entered the room and began to ask my mother a series
of questions. On and on the nurse continued until we were both
teary-eyed. We knew my sweet, precious mother was very weak and
needed immediate attention.

As I looked at her, so many memories flooded my mind. My
mother had always sacrificed her time and energy for me and loved
me unconditionally. She had never criticized me. One of my girl-
friends had once exclaimed that she wished she had my mother

instead of hers. My mother was a jewel, but I knew I was not the most caring or tactful daughter.

My brother and I stayed with her most of that day. Her cardiologist came to talk to us in the late afternoon. He and the orthopedic surgeon were hesitating to schedule surgery because they did not know if she could survive since she was so weak and her heart condition severe.

> *She looked beautiful to me. How could she be so sick and weak?*

That was terrible news. I felt that my mother would always be with me. She looked beautiful to me. How could she be so sick and weak that the doctor didn't want to perform the surgery?

Around seven that night, I did a stupid, thoughtless thing. I left for a rehearsal with my band. I never should have left her side. After the rehearsal ended, I made another stupid decision. Instead of going back to the hospital, I went home. I was tired and afraid to park and walk the dark path to the hospital.

Too Late to Say Goodbye

I did go back early the next morning, but only after receiving the call that my mother had died at 5:00 AM. I knew I would never forgive myself.

I was flooded with thoughts of things I wished I had done, but what good did it do now? It was finished. She had passed from this life to her glorious heavenly home, and I had not been there with her. I was the daughter she loved more than her life. I was the daughter she loved no matter how I disagreed with her or disobeyed her, but I felt I had disappointed her. I had not been with her to hug her and say goodbye.

Her funeral was amazing. The First Baptist Church was packed with people from all over the community who came to pay their respects. The altar was filled with flowers, because everyone loved my mother. She was a saint with a caring heart, full of love.

My late father and she had owned a hardware store, and I had repeatedly heard her listen to anyone's story of woe. People trusted her, confided in her, and often asked for her advice. She was a great comforter and adviser to many, including the young people she taught in Sunday school for years. I did not always follow her advice, because I often thought I knew better. Now, I realized I didn't, but it was too late to tell her.

> *I often thought I knew better. Now I realized I didn't, and it was too late to tell her.*

I was in despair after the funeral, blaming myself for neglecting her, but I went through all the things one does after losing a parent. My brother and I did the paperwork. We sorted clothes and items, wrote the cards, paid bills, and made sure everything at the cemetery was taken care of, and all the time I was grieving.

About four months after her death, I visited a friend in Nova Scotia. I arrived at a beautiful, weathered house near the sea and stayed in a Victorian bedroom with a fireplace and a cozy sofa. As the lights went out that night and I went to sleep, I don't know if I was dreaming, but I feel that I woke up and saw my beautiful mother sitting on the arm of the sofa with her sister, my sweet auntie, who had died only six months earlier.

They appeared as I had seen them in pictures when they were in their thirties. My mother had long raven hair and Auntie was a strawberry blond. Both had flawless skin and were wearing stylish clothes from that period when they were young. They were laughing and talking, as they had always done.

"Mother, I'm so glad to see you," I said.

She said, "Darling, I know. We have come because we want you to stop worrying. I know you've been worrying, but we are so happy and are having so much fun. This place is wonderful, and I have so many friends here. You know how much I love my sister, and now we are together again. I love you, my dear daughter, and I want you to stop worrying about me."

I started to say "I'm sorry," but my mother and aunt vanished, and only a dim light shone on the sofa for a moment. I had a wonderful, indescribable feeling as I went back to sleep.

The next morning, I told my friend what had happened, and we knew it was a miracle.

The nagging feeling that I should have done more for Mom in this life returned from time to time. A few months later, sometime after midnight, I saw my bedroom door open and a bright light shone. Mother entered and walked toward my bed. I sat up.

"Oh, Mother, thank God, I am so happy to see you. I love you so much. Oh, I wish you were here all the time."

My mother said, "I know, darling, but I came to tell you to please stop worrying. Everything is okay. Please do not worry about me. I am fine. I love you."

She was sitting on the edge of my bed so close to me. I felt her presence, and I wanted so much to embrace her as she was saying this. I reached to put my arms around her and hold her, but just then, she vanished.

My mother appeared to me one more time, when I was walking one warm, sunny day, soon after the previous appearance. I was overcome by her presence and the assurance that I had done enough in her lifetime. I knew everything was all right. I was sure I would be all right, and I knew she was happy.

> *I began to remember the good things I had done for her and the joyful times we shared.*

It took only a moment this time to relinquish my doubt and worry about what kind of daughter I had been. I began to remember the good things I had done for her and the joyful times we had shared. I was sure she had brought those remembrances back for me.

I don't understand the mystery, but I am thankful I had these visions or dreams or visits from my dear mother to comfort me and to tell me, "Don't worry about me."

Grieving Scott

ERIN DITTMAN

I have shied away from writing about my big brother, Scott, for years. Until recently, I couldn't understand the reason behind my fear. Now I know that writing about him made his death seem more real. And I wrestled with fears that he was gone forever, even though my faith assured me I would see him again one day.

The grief I felt regarding the loss of my brother was nothing that millions before me have not felt, but perhaps the way I gained healing was unique. I could go days or weeks, maybe even months, without thinking about Scott, but then when I heard a certain country song, I would go right back to the day he died. Or I could be watching an episode of a TV show and then sob uncontrollably when a scene reminded me of him.

Grief is like that; it ebbs and flows, and is as vast and as seemingly endless as the ocean. And just like a wave that comes out of nowhere, grief can knock us off our feet without a moment's notice.

When Scott died, we were estranged. The last twenty years of his life were difficult. He had struggled financially and had bought into one get-rich-quick scheme after another. He had mental issues and would self-medicate with alcohol and pills. He had an anger problem, so he would lash out at others. He had spent time at a homeless shelter in downtown Denver until he had been kicked out for drug use. The list went on and on, reading like a novel. I only wished it were fiction.

Scott's behavior had left our family in ruin. He had done all he could to alienate himself from me and my younger brother, Eric. He had used people for money, never intending to pay them back. My mom and dad had invested thousands of dollars in whatever they thought would make him happy, doing all they could to save him. In his wake, he had left a path of destruction, and, in the end, there was nothing any of us could have done for him.

In that moment, my anger vanished, and it never returned.

I had loved Scott, but there was a lot not to like. I had watched him taking more and more of my parents, leaving them as just shells of what they had been. He had robbed me of valuable time with my mom and dad. Before he died, they were so stressed nothing was left of them to salvage.

When Scott died of a drug overdose, not only did I lose my older brother, I also lost my mom, my dad, and the dreams of the perfect family I had always longed for. Scott and I would not grow old together, my kids would not know just how wonderful their uncle could have been, and our parents had to bury a son, blaming each other for his death. The anger I felt toward Scott, even after his death, seemed impossible to overcome.

I never got to make peace with him, never got to say goodbye. We hadn't spoken in a very long time, and I felt guilt and shame. It was devastating to lose someone when so much was left undone and unsaid. I wouldn't wish it on my worst enemy.

Months after his death I was grieving, clawing and scratching my way out of a very dark, deep hole. It was quite a journey.

On the Easter Sunday after he died, I listened as my pastor preached about heaven and the resurrection, but the words barely sunk in. Then, suddenly, everything faded from view, and I saw Scott in heaven, as real as day. I knew beyond any doubt that he was with God. All his pain was gone, all the things he longed for here on earth were no longer important. He was finally at peace, free of the pain and addiction that encumbered him.

In that moment, my anger vanished, and it never returned. It took many months, but I had thought it would take a lifetime! Only God can do something this amazing and miraculous. This change in my heart was one of the most powerful moments of my life.

It has been eight years since that Easter Sunday, and while the anger is gone, I still feel sadness for the loss and for what could have been, regret for all those years that Scott and I were estranged. I am brokenhearted for my parents. Sad to say, there are no earthly winners in this tragic story.

I'm also left wondering if we could have bridged the gap if we'd had more time. Alas, that is the question we all ask from time to time: *What if?* I read recently that the world does not cater to our timing.

Recently I remembered the words in that Easter sermon and seeing Scott in heaven. Tears ran down my face, the memories fresh and thick as I thought about that day and how I was delivered from so much. That, in and of itself, is a miracle.

After the tears, I smiled, remembering what a gentle soul Scott was, and realizing how much I adored my big brother and how very much he loved me. And I remembered how God took my feelings of deep grief and anger and showed me that Scott is fine, well, and healed, resting in His arms. I find great comfort in that and in the fact that I will, someday, be reunited with him when he welcomes me home. What a glorious day that will be!

The Black Dress

NANCY LEE JENKINS

B e quick about your son, for his time is short."
The message, at once frightening, disturbing, woke me from a sound sleep. I looked at the clock at my bedside. It was 3:00 AM. This voice spoke with such authority I had no doubt it was God speaking to me, demanding my attention. Questions filled my mind. I had three sons. Which one's life was at stake? And when would he be taken?

Already I felt overcome with grief. I turned to my husband, Joe, expecting that he, too, had heard the voice. But he was motionless, breathing deeply, as if nothing had disturbed the quiet of our night.

Quickly, I slipped out of bed, threw on my robe, and hurried to my sons' bedrooms. I went first to my youngest, Jeff, who was only nine. I begged God to spare him. He was the only child from my marriage with Joe; surely, this message could not be for him.

Then I moved to Larry's room, my oldest boy. Stroking his head, I parted the hair on his forehead and gently kissed his brow. Tears flowed as I tried to reason. Could the warning be for him? I prayed, "God save the soul of this child; don't let him be lost."

Suddenly I heard restless movement from the adjoining room and my thoughts raced. Charley! Of course—our difficult, rebellious, and strong-willed middle child. This message must be for him. I raced to his side.

It was all I could do to refrain from pulling him out of bed, to have him pray to ask God's forgiveness and invite Jesus into his heart. My heart was broken at the thought of losing any of my sons. My tears flowed as I prayed for God to have mercy on Charley.

Protect, guide, and lead him to You, Lord, I pleaded.

I could hardly wait for morning. Finally, the sun rose, but before I let the boys get dressed, I gathered them around me, praying for each of them.

> *I gathered them around me, praying for each of them.*

As soon as the boys were off to school, I phoned my pastor. I told him what had happened and that I had prayed throughout the night. He reassured me that even if one of my sons died in his thirties, it would be considered a "short" life. So maybe, he reasoned, it would be years. But I was certain the Lord had spoken to my heart to prepare my son and me for what would soon be reality.

A year passed. I had kept the message to myself, telling no one beyond my pastor, not even Joe. I strove to hug my boys more, to spend more time with them, to pray for them more. As I got in the habit of focusing on my boys as much as I could, the impact of the message started to fade. Maybe my pastor was right; maybe my sons would be alive for decades.

Then, one day, while I was shopping at my favorite boutique, I started sorting through the bargains on the clearance rack, and a black dress almost spoke out loud: "Buy me!"

As I reached to touch the material, I froze. A familiar voice from within said, "You will need this dress. Buy it."

My whole being silently screamed, "*No!* I don't want a black dress! I won't buy you, I won't!"

I almost yelled at the dress as I dashed out of the store, with my heart pounding. Sitting in my car, almost out of breath, I thought of how silly it was of me to get so upset over a dress. Why should a smart-looking dress send me into a tizzy almost to the point of panic just because it was black?

After I regained my composure, I began to talk to God, remembering the night of the power-filled voice. "It is coming soon, isn't it, Lord? He won't reach adulthood, will he? I'll need a winter black dress?"

> *I just wanted to go home and put my arms around my boys.*

In my spirit, I heard His soft reply, "Yes."

I no longer felt like shopping. I just wanted to go home, put my arms around my boys, and hold them.

Focusing on Loving My Sons

As I drove home, I wondered if I could somehow stall God's will. My daily routine of being wife and mother kept me busy enough that I didn't have time to dwell on a dress, especially a black one. I focused on my boys more than ever. Whenever the words of that early morning message came to my mind, I was spurred to draw close to them, to show them my love.

Then my shopping trips became troublesome again. When I visited a mall, that same black dress appeared on a mannequin in a store window. As I walked past, that dress seemed to whisper, "You can't get away from needing me."

About a year later in a shopping center of a different town, unbelievably, there was the same dress, marked down from fifty dollars to the irresistibly low price of eight dollars.

My soul cried out in despair, *Not here, too! Is there nowhere I can go to escape you?*

I fought the intrusions of that black dress. On the way home from shopping that day, I bought a plain black wool dress at a yard sale for twenty-five cents. Feeling the matter settled, I went about my daily routines, loving my sons more than ever, with God's warning slipping to the back of my mind again.

More than two and a half years had passed since I had heard God's voice. One cold February day, school was closed, and the boys were bored. Jeff wanted to go roller-skating, and I wanted to spend time with Joe. I offered to pay for all three boys to go skating if Larry, who was now driving, would take them.

The boys were very close. Larry and Charley loved their little brother and would do just about anything for him, so Jeff hardly had to ask them to take him. Off they went.

The Call I'd Dreaded

Joe and I went grocery shopping and were carrying the bags into the house when the phone rang. I ran to answer it.

"No!"

Joe dropped his bags at the sound of my scream. Groceries scattered down the sidewalk as he ran to me.

The caller from the hospital continued, "Is Jeff allergic to any medication? Do we have your consent to treat him for his injuries?

It's bad. We need you to come right away. I want you to be prepared for the worst."

This isn't happening. How? Where?

Click. The caller was gone.

Prepared. How that word resounded: *Prepared.*

"Is this what you were getting me prepared for, Lord? Tonight?"

He answered gently, "Yes, my child," as He welcomed our youngest son of eleven years into His heavenly kingdom. Jeff had been crossing a road when a car traveling forty-five miles an hour had thrown him eighty feet into the air.

> *It brought a great peace to have confirmation that heaven is a real place.*

As we drove home from the hospital with broken hearts, God suddenly opened my spiritual hearing, letting me listen to Jeff's voice exclaim, "Wow!"

I knew he was seeing his new heavenly home.

While we made the funeral arrangements, I reflected on that black dress. Yes, I did wear the yard-sale dress and then shoved it to the back of my closet until I totally yielded the pain and grief of our loss to God.

More than thirty years later, that black dress still hangs in my closet, reminding me of my personal struggle in trying to change God's will. I've learned over the years to accept God's provision without question. Now, I trust and receive whatever He has for my life, for only God knows what awaits our future. And thankfully, just as clearly as God warned me of impending grief on that 3:00 AM visit, He has provided other reassurances and moments of comfort.

A week after Jeff's funeral, I had a dream about the Gates of Pearl that encompass the City of God in heaven. They were magnificent:

huge pearls with the pure light of God, whiter than white with light shining over the top. It brought a great peace to my soul to have confirmation that heaven is a real place.

About ten years later, God gave me a vision in the form of a framed family picture. Jeff was standing in front of my grandma and my aunt, with each having a hand placed on Jeff's shoulder. As I saw this vision, peace comforted my soul, as if these much-loved women were saying, "We have him; he is with us. All is well."

Amazing Grace

SUSAN M. WATKINS

My dad felt strongly about extending kindness to others. When he lost his own father in the shadow of the Great Depression, he had two choices: become hardened by circumstances or remain flexible. Despite his young age, he opted to treat others the way he wanted to be treated. Though he was often bullied, Dad entered adulthood with his compassion intact.

Dad was my hero and I his shadow. Even though he didn't have the advantage of having a father's influence, my dad was a positive role model. His determination to provide me with a better childhood than his succeeded. His commitment and tenacity taught me invaluable lessons.

My father was athletic—from precision archery to high-diving and swimming. He could enter the water from thirty-three feet above and barely disturb the surface. Like a warm knife slicing softened butter, his dives were smooth and exceptional.

Still actively independent as a senior, Dad was on his way to mail bills when he tripped over a slight irregularity in the sidewalk. He broke his hip. After surgery, he asked me to move into his hospital room. The staff provided a chair that was best described as a sheet atop railroad tracks.

Dad had good and bad days. We sang together, laughed, and cried, keeping Dad's mind off his pain. Pneumonia settled in, and

I was told he would never regain his health. But with the many prayers lifted up, he did recover.

However, when he was preparing for discharge, he unexpectedly became comatose. I continued talking and singing his favorite song, "Amazing Grace," as I was certain he could hear me. The neurologist was astounded to discover that when I told Dad his favorite jokes, he would chuckle, and when I sang his favorite songs, he kept time with his foot.

Dad's case appeared in the *New England Journal of Medicine*, proving comatose patients were aware of their surroundings and could respond.

Within days, he regained consciousness.

One evening, Dad was focusing his attention at the foot of his hospital bed. He was pleasantly talking for several minutes with an unseen visitor. I knew

> *"Dad, were you speaking with an angel?" I asked.*

what was happening and remained quiet. He composed himself and asked if I saw them.

"Dad, were you speaking with an angel?" I asked.

"Oh yes," he affirmed.

"Dad, what were you told?" I asked.

"He said it wasn't time just yet. That they weren't coming for me right now, but it would be soon."

"Were you apprehensive or unsettled with the conversation?" I pressed.

"No, not at all. I still have more time."

I began fighting tears, and Dad immediately began to comfort me and assured me that everything would be fine. He reminded me that God was in control and would help me navigate this journey.

A few days later, Dad slipped into another coma and was transferred to hospice. I began to prepare myself emotionally. A lifetime of love kept me anchored, and I thought these were our last weeks together.

> *My loving golden retriever found my father's room by scent alone. They were best buddies.*

Dad shocked everyone by again regaining consciousness from this second coma. He was eating, taking medicine, and visiting with his extended family and friends for several days. Laughter echoed from his room for a week before he went into a third coma. The staff mentioned that pets were allowed to visit so I sent for Samson. My loving golden retriever found my father's room by scent alone. They were best buddies.

"Isn't That Nice?"

Samson sniffed around Dad's bed and then looked at me with an odd expression. My spiritually sensitive dog began trying to wake Dad. His hand was resting on the edge of his bed, and Samson kept bouncing against the bed, making Dad's hand airborne, while licking it and attempting to wake him.

To the family's shock, Dad began smiling and rubbing Samson's head, and then said, "Isn't that nice?"

Samson provided a few more licks before Dad became unresponsive. His grand-dog stood up on his hind legs, looked at him intently, and then sadly curled up under his bed.

Early the following morning, I awoke to incredible peace saturating our shared room. I knew the Lord's powerful presence was signaling it was time. Dad had a look of joyful expectancy. I knew he was silently preparing for the Lord to escort him to his eternal home. We had shared a time of extended prayer while he was still able. My father was ready. We had said everything necessary to one another, and right to the last he recounted his love for me, his family, and his Savior.

I held my father a final time and again softly sang those words he loved, "Amazing grace, how sweet the sound . . ." At last, I let go of his hand as his Master grasped the other. My immense sorrow was tightly laced with joy, knowing my father had just stepped into eternity and we would be permanently reunited one day.

I was tasked with emptying his home. Even though I knew his earthly journey was closing, it didn't prepare me for the weight of full grief. Such grief is proof of love. As I slid the key into his door, I desperately prayed for strength.

Wanting Dad's Comfort

It was dark inside, exactly as he had left it when taking his bills to the mailbox a month earlier.

The difficult realities of his absence released rivers of tears. The family patriarch was gone, and I was forced into unwanted change and acceptance. It was, of course, a challenge for everyone, but I had been involved in his daily medical care and had done everything possible to prolong his life—my focus ground to a brutal stop when Dad stepped into heaven. The abrupt halt was emotionally jolting.

Drying my eyes, I forced myself to get busy. I decided to begin in the kitchen. Seeing Dad's used dishes and uneaten food brought a new wave of crying, along with seeing my notes and comics he had placed on the refrigerator. More tears, then prayers, got me back on task. I began to wonder if I would get everything cleaned before the movers arrived to take his items away.

I brought Dad's portable radio into the kitchen to drown out my grief with music. Unfortunately, static jarred my ears. I extended the antenna but still could pick up no stations.

I was about to turn the radio off when suddenly "Amazing Grace" broke through the static and came in, crystal clear. This was so unexpected I stepped back and tried to analyze how it was possible. Immediately I realized it wasn't random.

> *Suddenly, "Amazing Grace" broke through the static and came in, crystal clear.*

I backed against the opposite counter and put my hands to my mouth, and I felt Dad's loving presence surround me. I knew he couldn't bear to see me so anguished and wanted to let me know all was well. His favorite song blaring from his radio was the only method he could communicate his love to me.

I thanked the Lord for His kindness and for binding my broken heart as only He could. My mourning turned into joy as I sang along with the cherished hymn. A full orchestra backed every stanza, a version that was completely new to me. I decided to listen to the station's deejay for details on the song.

However, when the last verse played and the final note faded, the radio emitted another loud crackle and static. I went to the radio, slowly turning the dial in both directions looking for the station. Only there wasn't a station. *Anywhere.* I carried Dad's radio all over his home looking for reception but found none.

Sinking into a chair, I realized what had just happened. No radio station was airing that song. There was no special arrangement of its recording. It wasn't a freak coincidence that right after I turned the radio on, I heard that particular song.

This music wasn't from earth.

Dad comforted me by using unconventional means: "Amazing Grace" was his signature song, and it helped dry my tears and ease my grief. I finished organizing his belongings with a completely revised perspective.

I still grieved my father's passing, but whenever I felt sad, I remembered that unique moment, and the cloud lifted.

Years later, I was telling my young grandson about his great-grandfather. I told him he would have loved playing with him, and that his very favorite song was called "Amazing Grace."

Contemplating those two words, he thought about them for a moment and then asked for clarification. "Amazing Grapes?" he questioned. I dissolved into laughter, knowing Dad would have roared with delight hearing his great-grandson's innocent mispronunciation.

In fact, he probably did.

The Angel's Promised Return

WANDA SUE HOLMES

My husband, Buddy, called the doctor to get the results from his biopsy. His voice trembled as he spoke.

"I'm calling," he said, "to get the results from my autopsy."

"No," I whispered, "your biopsy."

God knew we needed a laugh.

Together, we had been building our own home for many years. We kept working, even after Buddy retired, and looked forward to the day we could also retire our tools. We had plans to get away, travel, and enjoy life. Then, like a tsunami, pancreatic cancer invaded our lives, and it was no laughing matter.

Buddy had always been a quiet, loving, and patient man with a great sense of humor. His diagnosis changed him into a man with eyes that were cold, hard, and glaring. He tried to pick fights and snapped at me. But, underneath it all, I understood, he was *so* afraid.

We attended church together until close to the end. Buddy was no longer able to enjoy the service because of medical issues. But he drove me there and waited in the car. If he fell asleep, I would wake him gently after the service ended, and then we would talk about the sermon all the way home.

Eighteen long months after the devastating news, the doctor recommended hospice.

Buddy was still afraid. Although he knew he had cancer, he couldn't accept the possibility that he might die.

"If I get worse," he said, "I don't want to know. Promise you won't tell me? I don't want hospice taking care of me, either. I don't want The Death Watchers anywhere by me."

One morning, Buddy work up with a new gleam in his eyes.

I found myself digging for tissues repeatedly as I saw him sink deeper into himself every day. He didn't even want to watch television.

"Please God," I prayed. "Help him so he's not afraid to die."

I had to trick him into letting hospice come. I told him I wouldn't get them but that I would call in a registered nurse, because I needed someone to help out. I think he knew what I was up to, but by pretending he didn't, he could accept the situation. The kind and loving hospice workers were a godsend.

A Newfound Hope

One morning, Buddy woke up with a new gleam in his eyes, unlike anything I had witnessed for months.

"I'm going to heaven," he announced.

My breath suspended for a moment.

"Oh, you think you are?" I stammered.

"I *know* I am," he said with a strong, secure voice. "An angel came into my room last night. He stood at the foot of my bed and held his arms out. He was very large and wore a long white robe. I felt such *power in* the room, like nothing I had ever felt before.

He paused, and then went on. "I looked at him and said, 'I'm not ready yet.' The angel gave a beautiful white-toothed smile, then turned, and walked away. I'll be going to heaven in two weeks."

Buddy seemed calm and content. Something wonderful had happened to him. His whole countenance had changed.

"Are you afraid?" I asked.

"No," he said, showing his crooked grin.

"Thank You, God," I whispered with a joyful heart.

Buddy slept in the hospital bed from hospice.

He started talking and was full of questions about heaven.

"Hey, my precious," he said to me, "will you lie down with me?"

"You don't have much room in that bed, and I don't want to hurt you."

"You won't hurt me, and I need you. Come over here, please?"

His eyes looked peaceful. I climbed into his bed and snuggled beside him. He wrapped his now-skinny arms tenderly around me. I had desperately missed lying next to him. I brushed my cheek against his and whiffed that oh-so-familiar aftershave. I was afraid of hurting him, but nothing had ever felt so comfortable and good. He started talking and was full of questions about heaven.

"What if I can't find my way around there? What if I get lost?"

"You don't have to worry about that. The instant you get there, everything will feel like home. You'll get to see Jesus face-to-face. Your mother and my mother will be there. They'll probably get together and make one of their famous meals you always loved. And since your dad died when you were only five months old, you'll get to see him for the first time. Your sisters and brothers and my brother Rodney will be there waiting to welcome you home and show you around. Jesus has prepared mansions for two thousand years, and yours is finished. You won't have to worry about drywall or anything else about building ever again."

I kissed his cheek and felt his tears mingle with my own. We cuddled together for the longest time. Neither of us had to move. We didn't have to change positions. The telephone never rang, and neither one of us needed a bathroom break. We talked heaven for the entire time. That was truly God's special blessing to both of us.

"I'll be waiting for you, my precious, and I'll carry you over the threshold of the heavenly portals."

When I finally crawled off his little bed, three-and-a-half hours later, I felt like I could almost float. The pain that had surrounded my heart was so relieved. I could hardly wait to tell the kids everything Buddy had said.

After telling our son, Trevor, about Buddy's visit from an angel, I asked him, "What do you think? Do you think he's just been on too much medication? Or do you think he really had a visit from an angel?"

"Well," he said, "Dad was never a person to make things up, so yes, I believe him. I think it happened just like he said."

How could I ever doubt that God had answered my prayer?

A Husband's Love

Buddy's humor returned, and he seemed almost like his old self. The hospice staff went out of their way to support my husband.

"Is there anything you've always wanted to do, but haven't been able to? Is there anything you would like to see, or do, or have?" they asked him.

"Well, we did order some carpet for the living room," he said. "We were going to have it delivered so we could do it ourselves. I would like to see that installed." Hospice sent men over for the installation.

With the carpet laid, Buddy told them he would like to see the trim in the living room finished. Two men came and completed all the trim. Then he told them, "I would love to see the master bedroom covered with drywall."

> *"I'm trying to get the house finished for you, my precious."*

"We'll see what we can do," they said.

Buddy called me into the bedroom and then whispered in my ear. "I'm trying to get the house finished for you, my precious."

Our son came over to admire the improvements. His dad pointed them out from his bed, which we had moved to the living room.

"Hey, nice, huh?" Buddy proudly exclaimed. "Is there anything you need to have done over at your house? I can ask."

Trevor just smiled.

The hospice representative asked my husband if he would like someone to come over and give him a massage.

"Only if my wife can get one too," he said.

They agreed, but I didn't want to bother them. They stopped by every couple of days and gave Buddy a massage, gently, on his frail, aching body. He would tell them, "Well, that was a good rub."

Soon thereafter, the nurse called me aside. "Buddy has slipped into a coma. You should call in all the family to say goodbye."

Heartbroken, I called our pastor and told him.

"I'm on my way," he said.

Before the pastor got there, Buddy came back to us, opened his eyes, and started talking. Our pastor arrived and went in to see Buddy. He came out looking wide-eyed.

"I don't know what they told you," he said, "but *that's* not a coma."

This happened several times, and Buddy amazed everyone. The nurses agreed, "This just doesn't happen. They don't do that. I've never known anyone like that with a pulse so low who was still alive. He keeps going and going. We're going to call him the energizer Buddy."

He woke up one morning with a surprised look. "I'm still here?"

Whenever we asked him what he needed, he always pointed up and said, "Heaven."

Suddenly, reality hit me full force.

I'm going to lose my husband.

"Oh, God," I cried, "I can't do this, I just can't."

God seemed to say, "I'll help you."

My overwhelming sadness faded. I went back and stood at Buddy's bedside. He was weak but still hanging on as he hovered between this world and the next.

He had been in and out of consciousness, but he suddenly spoke two words, very clearly: "Dad, Dad."

I leaned over and kissed him on the lips. "I love you," I said. I felt his lips as he tried, with what little strength he had, to kiss me back. He could only mouth the words, "I love you too," and then he was gone.

It was exactly two weeks after his visit from the angel!

If we could have peeked into the unseen world, I'm sure we would have witnessed the angel standing at the foot of the bed again, with his arms stretched out. Only this time Buddy would have said, "I'm ready now."

Although pain and sadness filled my heart, God gave me the peace that passes all understanding. One day, in church, I was crying. Something told me to look up. When I did, I caught a quick glimpse of Buddy and heard him say. "Don't cry, my precious."

> *Another night I had a dream. Buddy looked young, handsome, and healthy again.*

Another night I had a dream. Buddy came to me, not in the body that cancer stole from him, nor the body with the speech impediment he had handled since childhood. His voice was crystal clear. No more dentures, but pearly white teeth. He looked young, handsome, and healthy again.

God is near to the brokenhearted. He sent many people to bring comfort and help me through my grief. Day by day, God eased my heartache, and life continued after I let my husband go.

PART 3

Devotions

*So also you have sorrow now, but I will see
you again, and your hearts will rejoice,
and no one will take your joy from you.*

—John 16:22 (ESV)

Witness of the Stained-Glass Lamb

I can do all things in him who strengthens me.
—Philippians 4:13 (RSV)

I sat alone on the hard pew of my church, gazing up at the lamb in the stained-glass window above the altar. Now the lamb's pure white coat was in shadow, as if Jesus Himself were grieving with me. I had last looked at the lamb in the window during the recent memorial service here for my husband, Jim, who had died in a plane crash at the age of 46. I bowed my head and shut my eyes.

I felt completely weak and drained of all energy, as if I could hardly lift my hand to open the Bible in the pew. I didn't see how I could possibly go on without Jim by my side. He should be sitting next to me right now. He was my best friend, lover, confidant, advisor, and playmate. I saw my life stretching ahead of me, empty. Maybe I should have been sitting beside him when the plane crashed.

Suddenly I lifted my head, as if a force were telling me to look up at the lamb. A sun shaft was coming through the stained glass and lighting the lamb with a strong, bright glow. As I looked at the light of the pure white lamb, I seemed to feel a new energy, as if the light itself were suffusing my body with strength. The luminous lamb looked triumphant, his head raised as if in defiance of death. I stared at the shining lamb for a long time; the sun shaft never dimmed. For the first time since Jim died, I felt sure he was safely in heaven with Jesus. Knowing that, I could now go on living.

Lord, when we are deeply in grief and feel as if we can no longer go on, You give us strength we didn't know we had. Thank You for never, ever forsaking us.

—PEGGY EASTMAN

Far from Home

If I rise on the wings of the dawn, if I settle on the
far side of the sea, even there your hand will guide me,
your right hand will hold me fast.
—Psalm 139:9–10 (NIV)

The news of my dad's imminent death came to me when I was 1,700 miles from home, working aboard a cruise ship. The ship docked in Tortola, British Virgin Islands, and I disembarked in deep sadness. I had no plan, just a map and three hours to wander, so I headed toward Main Street.

I stopped in front of a lovely white church with red shutters, red handrails, and a red cross above the entrance. A turn of a knob revealed an unlocked door. I stepped inside the empty church and sat down.

"Welcome," a man said. I had not noticed him sitting on a piano bench at the front.

"Oh, hello," I said. "I'm sorry to interrupt you." I stood to leave.

"Please, feel free to stay as long as you'd like. We're getting ready to have a worship service with the children from our school."

As if on cue, a side door opened. Children wearing green plaid uniforms filtered in and stood around me. The played a lively intro, and the children broke into joyful song: *Enter his gates with thanksgiving and his courts with praise; give thanks to him and praise his name. For the* LORD *is good and his love endures forever . . .* (Psalm 100:4–5 NIV).

My dad entered those gates a few hours later. Though I was far from home on a small island in the Atlantic Ocean, God encircled me with love and filled my heart with unspeakable joy. No matter where we are or what we are experiencing, God is close to us.

Dear God, thank You for being near me at home and far away,
when days are happy and when days are too hard to bear.

—BECKY ALEXANDER

Friendship's Sweet Aroma

For we are to God the pleasing aroma of Christ among those
who are being saved and those who are perishing.
—2 Corinthians 2:15 (NIV)

Spring was everywhere one morning as I walked alone in my neighborhood. A wren sang, and colorful daffodils and tulips painted the scene with bright reds and yellows. The whole world seemed to sing God's praises. All except me, that is.

I was still missing my close friend and walking partner Willa, who'd passed away unexpectedly only a week before. For days, I'd barely been able to climb out of bed. But today, I'd promised myself I'd get outside and exercise.

A dark cloud parked itself over the sun as I rounded the corner. I turned up my collar and stepped up my pace, hoping to make it home before the skies opened. Willa and I had walked this route many times, chatting or even singing favorite hymns. Now, daily strolls would feel so lonely.

Forcing myself to keep going, I passed a home with a fig tree on either side of the yard. As I gazed at the fig's large leaves, my heart ached. When Willa learned how much I love Fig Newton cookies, she'd baked a batch for me, using figs from the tree in her yard. Those cookies had been melt-in-your-mouth delicious and my mouth watered just thinking about the delicately spiced figs.

Just as I passed the fig trees, the sun popped out, and the heavenly smell of home-baked cookies wafted from an open window. I stopped and drew in deep breaths, drinking in the delicious aroma as I pictured Willa in my mind's eye, letting me know she was near. I rushed home, thanking God with a song in my heart, eager to bake cookies.

Lord, I want to be a pleasing aroma to You. When grief tries to isolate me, encourage me to experience the beauty and healing of the natural world—the world You created. I'll honor my departed loved ones with songs of praise to You.

—LINDA S. CLARE

Three Dates

You saw me before I was born. Every day of my life was recorded in your book. Every moment was laid out before a single day had passed. How precious are your thoughts about me, O God. They cannot be numbered!
—Psalm 139:16–17 (NLT)

For years, two dates have stood as a memorial to my son. The date God formed my son in my womb and the date he returned to heaven when I miscarried. No fanfare or services marked either occasion. Silence surrounded my pain. A loss bookmarked by the inability to let others in.

Time does not heal all wounds. I've watched as my other children grow, thankful for the blessing of motherhood. Yet I still grieve the loss of the child I have in heaven. Who would he look like? Would he have my eyes or his father's smile? Questions for which I will never know the answer, each an open wound.

Then there are moments when I catch a glimpse of heaven. Dreams of a little boy with familiar features. He is laughing and playing without a care in the world. This is when I am reminded of the third date. The day when I will be able to hold him in my arms. The day when we meet for the first time. When time and space no longer stand as a barrier between us, and we stand together in the presence of God.

Just as there was a date of conception and of his heavenly transition, there will be a date for our reunion.

Father, thank you for meeting me right where I am with open arms and loving me through the pain. You know me intimately and completely. Uphold me in my times of weakness. Be my strength when I have none.

—DR. SAUNDRA DALTON-SMITH

The Piano Tuner

Disease took my dad at the dawn of his retirement. I resented that he had died so young, when so many older people were enjoying life. Looking back, I can see this path was not a helpful one. That's probably why, four days after my dad died, God sent a 150-year-old man to my house to tune my piano.

Okay, he wasn't actually 150. But when I walked into the kitchen to look for my checkbook, that's how old I told my husband he was.

As I paid him, we made small talk. "Did you grow up here in town?"

The piano tuner began to tell me his story. Loss had punctuated his years. He shared a tragic event in his life that God had fully redeemed. Then he told me about a trial he was in the middle of. He teared up as he looked me in the eyes and said, "But this is what God does: He takes the sad, terrible things, and He turns them around and uses them for good."

He gently reminded me of the truth I knew in my head, but my heart had momentarily forgotten. I sobbed as I told him my dad had just died. By now, we were both blubbering. He offered me the comfort and wisdom of someone who had watched God's faithfulness in a broken world for almost nine decades.

I thought I'd hired this man to tune my piano. It turned out God had sent him to tune my heart.

Who am I to question the number of days the Lord allowed me to enjoy my dad? What an immeasurable blessing to have called Dennis my father. Thirty-five years with him was a priceless gift from a good God.

Father, please continue to remind our broken hearts that we have an eternal hope—free of suffering, tears, or pain.

—MOLLY DEFRANK

Overflowing Grace

But he said to me, "My grace is sufficient for you,
for my power is made perfect in weakness. . . ."
—2 Corinthians 12:9 (NIV)

Eight years ago, I sat across from Susan, glasses of iced tea and chicken salad sandwiches in front of us. A rare lunch date with an old friend.

After a while, she confided, "Lori, I'm worried about Bill. He's making bad choices."

Like her, I had concerns about my own son, Russell, also a young adult struggling to find his way. I encouraged her, "I really believe God's grace will cover our children, and us, no matter what happens. We have to trust God." At the time, I had no idea how much those words would echo in my head for years to come.

Three months later, I lost Russell. Consumed by a dark depression he had hidden from all of us, he committed suicide—a blow that rocked the foundation of our lives.

In the immediate aftermath of his death, my faith was shaken. Yet the words I had spoken to my friend spun in my mind like a whirlwind. Over time, even as I questioned God about this unfathomable loss, I began to understand He hadn't abandoned our family in our abyss of grief. People prayed for us. Others contacted us through phone calls, texts, emails, all reminding us we are not alone.

God has used our friends and family to shower us with overflowing love and grace. We will always struggle with grief, but we have also witnessed God's grace manifested through relationships that continue to strengthen us in our weakness.

Lord, Your grace, given freely by others acting as Your hands and feet on earth during our brokenness, has indeed been sufficient.

—LORI DURHAM

The Early Bird Gets the Worm

The soul of the sluggard craves and gets nothing,
while the soul of the diligent is richly supplied.
—Proverbs 13:4 (ESV)

My grandma had Alzheimer's, which robbed her of all parts of memory, leaving her unresponsive and unable to communicate. Our yearly family reunion tradition moved from visiting her at home to going to where she was being cared for. During these visits I wished I could speak with her. As a young adult, I used to be enamored with amazing stories she told me as a child. They revealed fascinating information about my Mom's childhood. As a teenager, I had my share of chances to have these conversations with Grandma. Instead, I scoffed at having to take another "hot drive down south."

At Grandma's funeral, a man who looked to be well into his nineties ambled into the funeral home with a much younger man on his arm. He tried to get everyone's attention as he pointed toward my grandma and said her name. He also kept saying "Billy." Everyone was struck with grief and didn't seem to notice the men. Shortly, they left. Almost instantly I remembered Grandma's many stories of working on Mr. Billy North's farm. I wondered if he was Billy. He must have pictures or stories of Grandma I'd love to see and hear. I wanted to bolt up and run after them. Unfortunately, I didn't.

All these years later I deeply regret not taking the time to speak with Grandma more often and neglecting to go after "Billy." These lost moments taught me the importance of urgency. These days, I rarely miss moments to connect with a loved one.

God, thank you for giving me the blessing of another day and the
chance to see the gratitude in all things good and bad. Thank you for
the lessons I am open to receive.

—ADRIENNE FARR

Coach's Favorite Song

I will . . . teach you in the way you should go;
I will counsel you with my loving eye on you.
—Psalm 32:8 (NIV)

Name the sport, Mike could coach it. The only thing he loved more than a ballgame was children. He had two of his own who, not surprisingly, excelled in every sport they played.

Mike had hundreds of other kids, too, kids he'd coached over many years. He taught them the rules of sports—and life. Be on time. Practice. Do your best. Play fair. Be a good loser. Be a good winner. Never give up.

Baseball was the sport Mike loved best. He knew the game inside and out. He was my son's Little League coach when he was in sixth grade. Mike's ragtag team of twelve-year-olds won the district championship. They won the regional championship. Then it was on to the state tournament, where his team won the final game—and the championship—in the bottom of the last inning. It was a summer none of those boys, or their coach, would ever forget.

But as fall came on, something puzzling happened to Mike. He lost his energy. He lost his appetite. He began leaving work early to go home for a long nap. Finally, he went to the doctor. The diagnosis was Stage IV lung cancer. Three weeks later, Mike passed away.

The church was packed for his funeral. Prayers were lifted up. Hymns were sung. Friends shared memories. And then the pastor said, "I usually discourage anything but sacred music at a funeral. But today, out of love for Mike, I hope you'll join in singing his favorite song." Then the organist played "Take Me Out to the Ball Game."

We all sang and cried tears of joy, because we knew our beloved coach was singing along with us, having slid in safe to his heavenly home.

Thank You, Lord, for those who love and lead our children.

—JENNIE IVEY

The Butterfly

*The Lord will rescue me from every evil attack and
will bring me safely to his heavenly kingdom.
To him be glory for ever and ever. Amen.*
—2 Timothy 4:18 (NIV)

Mom had lived with us, and every morning since spring she had said, "Let's go see what's blooming in your flower garden today." Then she was hospitalized and kept so heavily sedated that we couldn't communicate with her. I couldn't say goodbye before she died.

When my husband David and I drove home from the hospital to the September splendor of my flower garden, my heart ached knowing Mom would never sit there with me again.

I thought back to our time together in the garden. Bees and butterflies flitted from flower to flower as we sat on a bench in the garden. These visits became our best times together.

"Many people believe the monarchs represent the miraculous transformation our bodies make when we enter heaven," I had told Mom. She tried to get a closer look at the black and orange beauties, but they flew away.

Now I walked onto our deck, but before I opened the door, David said, "You have a butterfly on your head."

I turned and looked at my reflection in the glass. It was a monarch. "Wow! A butterfly has never landed on me like this."

I felt a warm sensation. "God, are You telling me Mom is in heaven now?"

The butterfly lingered on me for a few seconds and then gently flew away. I felt Mom was waving a loving goodbye to me.

Dear Lord, thank You for my mother who loved and nurtured me all my life. And thank You for the confirmation that her ill body will be transformed in heaven with You.

—CONNIE LOUNSBURY

Holding Lucky

He shall gather the lambs with his arm,
and carry them in his bosom. . . .
—Isaiah 40:11 (KJV)

O h, Lucky, what's wrong?" I asked, picking up my darling puppy, barely six weeks old. Shaking and crying, he burrowed into my arms as I hugged him and sat down in the rocker.

Poor little guy. Just the day before, at an area livestock auction, I'd stopped behind the cattle pens where a pile of black-and-white puppies rolled around together. The wife of an auction employee was selling a litter, though she planned to keep a couple for herself. We've had border collies for years. Shortly before my husband, Milton, passed away, we had unexpectedly lost our Laddie. The double loss sent me careening. Every day I shook uncontrollably while trying to hide it from everyone.

Still watching the puppies, I swung my leg over the low wire fence and sat on the ground. One puppy came over and plopped on my leg. Another skidded to a stop, jerked up, and then dashed away. And one caught my heart.

"That one," I said to the woman selling the puppies, pointing at my favorite. "I'll take him."

Now here in my rocker, he was scared and lonely, feeling lost without his boisterous brothers and sisters. Uncontrollable shivers ran through little Lucky as he snuggled closer. "You're all right, Lucky," I promised. "I've got you. There's nothing to worry about."

And suddenly I realized . . . this is what Jesus is doing for me. I'm crying and shaking and so afraid since Milton died, and He is holding me in His arms and telling me it's going to be all right. Peace swept through me. And my shaking stopped.

Thank You, God, for picking me up and never letting go.

—WANDA ROSSELAND

At Home with the Lord

It will be good to be at home with the Lord.
—2 Corinthians 5:8 (NLV)

I was thumbing through the mail when the contents of an unsealed envelope fell to the ground : two tickets to my favorite Broadway musical, *Les Misérables*. Clearly a surprise from my husband. I couldn't wait!

However, by the time the evening of the performances arrived, my desire for entertainment had waned significantly. My paternal grandfather, PeePaw, had been placed in hospice care, and I worried about missing what could be his final hours.

My family insisted we keep our plans, and from the orchestra's first note I easily became swept up into the story and the struggles of the characters. I had seen the musical several times before, but with my grandfather on my mind, I had never been so moved by the ending.

In his final scene, the main character, Jean Valjean, lies on his deathbed praying for God to take him home to heaven. He has lived a long, happy life serving the Lord and blessing others, and now he is ready to say goodbye to this life so he can rest at last in God's presence.

I openly sobbed as I watched the actor's flawless performance of the righteous Valjean and couldn't help but imagine my grandfather whispering the same prayers for eternity. PeePaw had blessed so many. He had lived and loved well. How close he was to his final reward.

We returned home late that night to a message from my parents. PeePaw had died around ten o'clock that evening, the same moment Valjean had sung his last notes on stage. I smiled. I hadn't missed PeePaw's final hours after all; I'd just experienced them in my heart through music.

Heavenly Father, thank You for Your perfectly timed reminders that my loved ones are at home with You in eternity.

—EMILY E. RYAN

Never Alone

For the LORD *your God is a merciful God;*
he will not abandon . . . you.
—Deuteronomy 4:31 (NIV)

Aunt Barb stared ahead, waiting for the stoplight to turn green, and announced, "God and I have an understanding. He leaves me alone, and I leave Him alone." I knew her opinion of God, but hearing her speak it was chilling.

For twenty years, her statement grieved me. When she was diagnosed with terminal cancer, my grief—and her bitterness—deepened. What comfort could I offer? I relied on actions rather than words. I placed a devotional and a bookmark on her coffee table. Each visit, I noticed the bookmark placed deeper into the devotional. Was she reading it?

As she grew weaker, so did her anger. She finally accepted God's gift of grace, but she was filled with fear. She asked what dying would be like. I chose the words I prayed would comfort her most. "When you open your eyes, Jesus and Grandma will be waiting for you."

A week later, my aunt slipped into unconsciousness. A hospice nurse stayed with us through the night. Just as dawn broke, the nurse's voice startled me. "Is she smiling?"

My aunt's face was turned toward me. She was smiling! Her mouth moved as if she were talking! To Jesus? To Grandma?

After she took her last breath, I asked the nurse, "How did you know?"

"She raised her hand and waved to someone. I've seen this before," she said.

Aunt Barb received a heavenly welcome, and I received a heavenly assurance. In spite of the years she left God alone, He did not leave her alone.

Thank You, Father, for promising to never leave me alone, not in life and not in death.

—KAREN SARGENT

Our Last Conversation

Set your hearts on things above, where Christ is,
seated at the right hand of God. Set your minds
on things above, not on earthly things.
—Colossians 3:1–2 (NIV)

I didn't realize Melissa, my best friend, was near the end of her life when I visited her in the hospital. Our conversation bounced from Melissa's twelve grandchildren to my daughter's pregnancy. "My goal is to get well enough to attend Cassie's baby shower," Melissa said.

When it was time to say goodbye, I hugged her and left. That was our last conversation. She unexpectedly slipped into unconsciousness the next day and passed away.

Wanting to preserve every memory of my sweet friend, I reviewed our last conversation over and over in my mind. What I pictured, of course, was Melissa in that hospital bed. And then, a truth of great magnitude rose in my heart: Melissa was not in a hospital bed—she was in heaven!

A few days before Cassie's baby shower, a gift-wrapped box appeared on my front porch. The attached card was from Melissa's daughter.

Dear Becky,
Mom wanted more than anything to attend Cassie's baby shower. She had already purchased these six outfits for the baby. She loved you so much, and I know she is celebrating in heaven. —Sherry

By setting my heart on things above, I'd allowed the reality of heaven to rise within me. By setting my mind on things above, God had shown me joy and hope even in the midst of grief and separation.

Dear God, help me move my focus from earthly things to the shining things above, in the place You have prepared for me and for those I love.

—BECKY ALEXANDER

Dream Time

Can any one of you by worrying add a single hour to your life?
—Matthew 6:27 (NIV)

On New Year's Day, I stood at my kitchen window, phone in hand. Although my first husband and I had divorced decades ago, his mom still called me every New Year's. I always told her how much I worried about her son as he tried to break into the Nashville music scene. On those calls she said, "Don't worry about him. God will take care of him."

As the day wore on, no call came. Maybe my former mom-in-law had moved on with her life. But I couldn't shake the feeling that something really was wrong. The night before, on New Year's Eve, I'd had a dream about my ex. In the dream, we sat next to one another. "You know," he joked, "we should've just been friends." Then he added, "Please don't worry about me—I'm with God, and I'll be okay." I couldn't get past a feeling that the dream seemed so real, but as the day went on, I was distracted by other things.

Three months after that New Year's dream, his mother called. At first, I was puzzled. Why would I hear from her after all this time? She said, "Dale passed away on New Year's Eve. I thought you'd want to know."

I offered my condolences and told her about the dream I'd had. "He said don't worry. He said he'll be okay." His mother thanked me for the assurance. We cried together before she hung up. Then it hit me: the dream happened the night he died. He was only forty-two.

I will always believe God sent my ex-husband's spirit to comfort me. I don't worry as much these days, knowing God's taking care of us all.

Lord, our times are in Your hands. I don't always know why friends and loved ones are called home. Let me learn to trust in Your timing, and let my dreams always reassure that You take care of us all.

—LINDA S. CLARE

Wings of Comfort

He will cover you with his feathers. He will shelter you with his wings. His faithful promises are your armor and protection.
—Psalm 91:4 (NLT)

Change came silently without any warning that my norm was being unraveled. My loved one's unexpected death left behind a wake of questions no one could answer. It was during this time of unbearable discomfort when I found the God of all comfort.

It was one week after the final goodbyes. The potted peace lily sat neglected in the corner, needing a deep watering. My soul was equally as dry. Disappointment surrounded me, keeping me held within my sorrow and pushing away the support of well-meaning friends.

Each morning was an act of obedience. Arising was a daily chore I forced myself to check off the to-do list. Coffee in hand, I made my way to my desk chair overlooking the yard. Life continued as if it didn't even notice the void that was left behind.

Then I heard it: the rustling of wings flapping.

Bright red feathers gently tapped on the window before retreating to a nearby tree branch. I watched the cardinal as it watched me—each staring at the other in wonder. Then it was gone. A chance spotting that lasted no more than a few minutes, or so I thought.

For over a month, it visited me each day, announcing its return with wings against my windowpane. Each morning watching over me. Each morning reminding me of God's closeness, faithfulness, love.

Now each time I see a red bird, I am reminded of God's wings of comfort.

Lord, You sought me when I did not have the strength to seek You. Thank You for Your faithful promises.

—DR. SAUNDRA DALTON-SMITH

Conduits of Comfort

The God of all comfort . . . comforts us in all our troubles,
so that we can comfort those in any trouble with the
comfort we ourselves receive from God.
—2 Corinthians 1:3–4 (NIV)

My dad's death was imminent, and I was tending to my five small kids, 200 miles away. I tried to ensure full tummies and to referee sibling brawls, but my heart was broken. I was a shell of a mom.

My mother-in-law came over to help. She kept a watchful eye on the kids and listened while I poured out my heart to her. I recalled memories of Dad that broke my heart: his timely puns, the clop-clop of his hush-puppy slippers walking around the house, the way he would listen to every long, boring story I'd ever told him. Tears choked my words as the memories gushed out.

She listened quietly for a long time. And then she said, "One day, these memories that are making you so sad right now will make you very happy."

This is a woman who has known grief intimately. A car accident took her husband at twenty-six, leaving her with two small children. Her words planted a seed of hope in my heart amid the pain.

Eight months after my dad's passing, those memories are slowly turning into tiny sparks, lighting flickers of joy in my heart (even if they do still set my tear ducts a-flowing).

I know now that God was using His people to minister to my broken heart. My mother-in-law was a conduit for His comfort.

I've since had the privilege of reaching out to friends who lost their parents. God's love is at work, even in the midst of deep sorrow.

Lord, thank You for Your people, who You use to speak life into death, comfort into pain. Give us eyes to recognize Your hand at work, even in our deepest mourning.

—MOLLY DEFRANK

The Gift

For God does speak—now one way, now another—though no one perceives it. In a dream, in a vision of the night, when deep sleep falls on people as they slumber in their beds.
—Job 33:14–15 (NIV)

Not long after my son, Russell, died, our daughter, Allison, twelve years younger than her brother and a freshman in high school, struggled with "survivor's guilt." She was consumed by thinking she could have prevented her brother's suicide, even though logic told her there was nothing she could have done. He had hidden his depression from all of us.

Her world was shattered. Unable to cope on her own and struggling to accept our family's "new normal," she retreated into her own thoughts. She sank into depression. She began to cut herself. But unlike her brother, she let us know she needed help. Through a combination of counseling and medication over the course of several years, she began to flourish once more and found hope for her future.

Shortly after Russell's death, God gifted Allison with an intense dream. In it, she was able to hold him, as if he were in physical form. He told her he only had a short time to be with her, but he answered her questions. The exchange has encouraged me through the years.

Allison asked, "What is it like?" and he replied, "It's like a blanket in the clouds. We sit there at a beach drinking iced tea."

No one on earth knows what heaven is truly like, but in moments when I miss my son the most, I think of him sitting on a blanket of clouds, watching the ocean of time roll in and out, surrounded by family and friends drinking iced tea and waiting patiently for the rest of us to join them.

Lord, thank You for speaking to us in dreams. They provide us with hope and encouragement when darkness surrounds us.

—LORI DURHAM

Love and Legacy

Children are a heritage from the LORD,
offspring a reward from him.
—Psalm 127:3 (NIV)

He's waiting for Jenna," my brother-in-law said. He, my husband, his other siblings, and I sat in the hospital room, watching what we thought would be their dad's last breath.

Family had surrounded Jim's bedside since he was admitted to the hospital after his last dialysis procedure. His body was too weak to continue treatments. For several days, Jim teetered between coherency and confusion, his body between life and death.

Jim's life revolved around God, faith, and his family. He was happiest surrounded by his children and grandchildren, as he was now. As each child and grandchild visited him for the last time, he pulled him or her close, one by one. The room felt sacred as Jim shared his final words with each one. Over two days, all twelve grandkids had seen Jim, except Jenna, who was out of the country as a missionary. She was flying home the night we all sat watching his shallow breathing. We didn't expect her to see him alive.

Though unresponsive for hours, he suddenly awoke that night, asking for his family. It's as if he knew Jenna was on her way. When she arrived, he was alert and ornery. They laughed and cried. Thirty-six hours later, he passed away.

Jim's tangible love in those final days mirrors the legacy he left. His love for God and family was undeniable. Though his absence seems too big sometimes, his heritage of life and love remains among us when we gather as a family. It almost feels as if he's there, too, binding us together.

God, thank You for the heritage of life that lives beyond death.
Help us to love well, not taking our family for granted. Equip us with
your peace that rests with us and among us.

—BRENDA L. YODER

Fields of Green

I am the resurrection and the life. The one who exercises faith in me, even though he dies, will come to life.
—John 11:25 (NWT)

Asmall whisper came from somewhere that said I should leave my desk and go to the hospital. A little while later my mom called, stammering out her words. "I don't know . . . uh, how to say this . . . Your daddy passed away."

I was a rock when I went to see his body and in the days leading up to planning the funeral. But afterward, complete and utter emptiness enveloped me. Where is he? How could such a loud, large man just be gone? My best friend had lost her mom a couple of years before and visited the grave frequently. She suggested I do the same, but I had no desire to. "He's not there," I'd say. "I wish I believed he was there, but I just don't."

"Please God, get me through this." After a short while, I kept having a vision of my dad running up a hill in a field of beautiful green grass. He was so happy, running toward me, leaping up the hill, arms swinging swiftly. I had this vision over and over, and at first it filled me with sadness and longing.

Finally I realized this vision matched so many pictures of what I learned paradise looks like. Vast fields of green, lost loved ones running into each other's arms after being resurrected, blissful joy and happiness. When I came to understand this vision, I thanked God continuously. My prayers were being answered, and I didn't even realize it. Although I could find no comfort in visiting my dad's grave, I certainly could in knowing he is safe and happy in heaven.

God please continue to bless me with openness and faith so I can hear Your answers. Thank You for Your ransom sacrifice and the promise of the resurrection.

—ADRIENNE FARR

Safe in His Mother's Arms

As a mother comforts her child, I will comfort you. . . .
—Isaiah 66:13 (NIRV)

My small town in Tennessee is reeling from a devastating tornado that touched down in the middle of the night. It destroyed more than two hundred homes and took nineteen lives. Among those killed were a young couple and their two-year-old son. Three deaths, but only two burial boxes. The child shared a coffin with his mother, her arms wrapped tight around him.

I have a hard time shaking that image from my mind. The couple were young and vibrant, devout Christians who loved their family, their community, and the Lord. Their world revolved around their precious little boy. As I try to process the tragedy, I can't help but wonder how many millions of parents and children, over the centuries, have died together.

It never occurred to me that many of them were almost certainly buried with a parent. Perhaps both parents, if a casket wasn't used. Who better to carry a child to eternity than the people who loved that child more than anyone on earth?

I'm a historian. I visit old cemeteries whenever I get the chance. Sometimes I make rubbings of the headstones. Tombstones of children are heartbreaking, but they're also interesting. They're little and oftentimes topped with a small statue of a lamb. Along with the child's name and dates of birth and death, I frequently find these words: *Safe in the Arms of Jesus.*

I don't know what's carved on the tombstone of the mother and child who died in the tornado. But I like to think it might be this: *Safe in the Arms of Jesus and Each Other.*

Because I know they are.

Lord, grant us comfort in tragedies we can't understand.

—JENNIE IVEY

When I Grow Old

May your unfailing love be my comfort,
according to your promise to your servant.
—Psalm 119:76 (NIV)

My sister Donna and I had been taught to act like proper ladies with good manners and quiet ways, but after Donna's diagnosis we discovered Jenny Joseph's poem, "Warning," which begins, "When I am an old woman, I shall wear purple."

In that poem, an ode to nonconformity, Joseph agrees that while we must ordinarily act according to society's norms, when we grow old, we may make up for our youth by wearing clothes that don't match, spending our money on nonessentials, and acting silly. For instance, when we grow old, we may run a stick along a public fence. Donna decided that would be our guiding principle now because she wouldn't live long enough to grow old. One day I told her, "Donna, I love you so much! I will never forget you."

"I love you, too," she said. "And you'd better not forget it, or I'll wake you at night with a rattle of my stick against a rail fence!"

After her funeral, my tears for her suffering and pain became tears for my own loneliness. "Lord," I prayed, "help me stop crying all the time."

The next morning, I awoke at dawn to what sounded like a rattle of a stick against a rail fence. It took me a moment to realize God was reminding me that Donna had loved me. She would want me to act outrageously now—to practice before I got old, just like the poem advises. "Thank You, Lord," I said, as I skipped to my closet to find something purple to wear with my red hat that wouldn't match.

Dear Lord, thank You for Your care and comfort, even when I come to You with the smallest requests. You are my rock and my shield, and I love You.

—CONNIE LOUNSBURY

Prepared for Trials to Come

Let us then with confidence draw near to the throne of grace, that we may receive mercy and find grace to help in time of need.
—Hebrews 4:16 (ESV)

I knew my mom had cancer before the doctors did. I sat in a college chapel service, mascara streaking my face. My parents had promised to call the minute they heard from the hospital. Overcome by what-ifs, I desperately prayed for a word from God. I just didn't expect one so clear.

Your mom has cancer, but she will not die from this.

The voice was quiet and steady. Like the roar of a lion and the simultaneous puff of gentle wind, the assurance flowed inexplicably around my chest. I knew the One who had spoken, and His comfort washed my fears.

Ten years later, I sat by my mom's bedside, saying my goodbyes. Her cancer had been stubborn, but she'd been in remission for years. True to His promise, it wasn't cancer that was pulling her home to her Saviour, it was the rest of her struggling body.

As I held her hand, that quiet whisper of peace came flooding back. This farewell was what He'd prepared my heart for so many years earlier. Wrapped in the tiny promise in a college chapel was the opportunity to see the incredible faithfulness of God throughout the years. He'd given us an extra ten years and been there through it all.

Goodbyes are never a part of our plan. And yet, as my mom passed into glory, I knew I was not alone. From the start, He'd been by my side, preparing and teaching me to rely on Him. For whatever tomorrow brings, I can rest assured it is seen and held by Him.

Thank You, Father, for Your faithfulness. As we look back and see Your presence throughout our lives, we praise You for guiding and drawing our hearts to You. Even here, on our darkest days, You are with us.

—LIZ MANNEGREN

Sadness Is Messy

In the multitude of my anxieties within me,
Your comforts delight my soul.
—Psalm 94:19 (NKJV)

How can a minivan get so disgusting? I surveyed the crushed Cheerios on the floorboard and the mystery liquid hardening in the cup holders and whispered an anxious prayer. *Where do I begin, God?* The car was one of many things I'd neglected over the past several weeks of grief and mourning for my late brother-in-law, Jared, who took meticulous care of his vehicles. He'd be so disappointed in me.

I was in the back row, hunched over a booster seat, digging candy wrappers out from the cracks, when I saw it. Large, scratchy writing, in pen, on the back of my tan leather seats. I almost came unglued.

Clearly, it was my daughter's writing, but I couldn't make out what it said. I called her outside and asked, in my most contrived calm voice, if she knew anything about the pen marks. Her face crumbled into a mess of tears. "I couldn't help it," she sobbed. "I'm sorry."

"But what does it say?" I asked, softening at her sorrow. These were more than the crocodile tears of a child caught in mischief.

"It says I miss you," she said with a hiccup. "I tried to clean it, but it won't come off." I pulled her close and stroked her hair. "I wrote it when we left the cemetery after Uncle Jared's funeral," she said. "Are you mad?"

Instantly, I felt God's peace. "No, baby, I understand," I assured her and knew in my heart that even Jared would understand as well. "Sometimes our sadness is messy."

The crushed Cheerios could wait another day.

Lord, sometimes I feel like I can fix my messy sadness by cleaning things around me. Remind me that feeling out of control and untidy is a temporary, but natural, part of grieving.

—EMILY E. RYAN

Forever Friends

As the Father has loved me, so have I loved you.
Now remain in my love.
—John 15:9 (NIV)

Sunlight filtered through the windows in the living room, where a hospital bed was placed so Mom could watch the birds. When the hospice chaplain arrived, I woke her. "All the people are here," she said.

I had read the hospice literature and suspected what was happening. "What are they doing, Mom?"

"Packing. I'm going on a trip." The chaplain and I exchanged glances.

Mom asked to sit up. Her eyes were more alert but clearly troubled. "I'm not ready. I have to see Sharon." They not seen each other in weeks, and I agreed to call her. The chaplain quietly asked me to call the hospice nurse as well. Physical signs indicated Mom was "actively dying."

Within an hour Sharon sat at Mom's bedside. The friends cried together, then laughed together, promising to find each other in heaven. Suddenly, energy surged through Mom. She listed more friends for me to call. Soon, people filled the room, and Mom chattered away. The hospice nurse arrived to find Mom hosting a party!

"This isn't unusual," the nurse explained. "Sometimes patients rally and become more engaged with their loved ones as the end nears."

For four days Mom pushed her walker through the house, checked email, and said funny things to make me laugh. Then the next morning the rally was over. "Hold my hands," Mom said. I sat beside her bed and warmed her chilled fingers. She smiled, so content. "I love my family and friends."

Mom spent her last days the same as she'd spent all the days before—loving people and being loved in return.

Thank You, Father, for loving us through our family and friends.

—KAREN SARGENT

A Crumpled Paper

The LORD is close to the brokenhearted and saves
those who are crushed in spirit.
—Psalm 34:18 (NIV)

Jarett? A wreck? No, no, no," I stammered. Rain pounded the window by my bed as I tried to fully wake up and comprehend the words coming through my phone. Less than a mile from my cousin Jarett's house, on a familiar yet dangerous curve, his Jeep hydroplaned on the wet road and hit a tree, killing him instantly. He was nineteen.

Six months passed, and the heartbreak seemed to increase for my Aunt Gail. With her son's twentieth birthday only two days away, she didn't know if she could bear it. Forcing herself to handle everyday tasks, she sat down at her desk to pay some bills.

Aunt Gail rummaged through the desk drawers to find a stapler. Her fingers ran across a crumpled paper at the back of the bottom drawer. She pulled it out and opened it. It was a letter . . . in Jarett's handwriting:

God's Love in My Life
John 3:16 says, "For God so loved the world, that he gave his only begotten Son, that whosoever believeth in him should not perish, but have everlasting life." I believe this is true, and I try to live by these words.

Proverbs 8:17 says, "I love them that love me; and those that seek me early shall find me." I love the Lord, and I found God's love. He has done great things in my life.

Just when Aunt Gail needed it most, God guided her fingers to it, assuring her that Jarett was safe in His care.

Dear God, thank You for the "crumpled papers" I find in my life.
They remind me You are close, especially when I have a broken heart.

—BECKY ALEXANDER

182

Lost and Found

"For this son of mine was dead and is alive again;
he was lost and is found." So they began to celebrate.
—Luke 15:24 (NIV)

I stood on the school playground, waving a metal detector across the deep, new-fallen snow. My eight-year-old daughter had lost her eyeglasses, and although I tried not to be angry with her, my emotions were on edge. Only a week before, I'd lost my best friend Patti to an aggressive cancer.

As I tromped around the white-blanketed playground, I told my daughter the chances of finding her spectacles were very slim. She began to cry. I bit my lip to keep from blubbering too—Patti's death had left a giant hole in my life and in my heart.

Years before, when we'd both lived in Southern California, Patti and I took her old VW van to the beach. That day, her wedding ring had slipped off her finger. We sifted through endless piles of sand but came up empty. Patti grabbed my hand and stared at me with her beautiful ice-blue eyes. "Let's pray."

After the amen, we had searched until sunset. With the light fading, we packed our things to go. Neither of us spoke. I hefted a large beach bag into the van, stopping to lean against the edge of the storage compartment. I looked down and there it was: Patti's ring, bright against the dark interior.

Now, I put my arm around my daughter. "Let's pray." We asked for God's help in finding her glasses despite the snow. I swung the metal detector again, and it erupted in urgent beeping. My daughter pawed through the white stuff and held up her glasses. We both thanked God for help as she wiped snow off her lenses. My best friend might be gone, but I felt her warm presence all around me.

Lord, it's so hard to lose those we love. Help me watch for the comforting little nudges that bring peace.

—LINDA S. CLARE

A Little Taste of Heaven

Taste and see that the LORD is good; blessed is the
one who takes refuge in him.
—Psalm 34:8 (NIV)

Each holiday reminds me of my grandmother's absence. I would arrive early for our family gatherings to enjoy extra time with her. Stained recipe cards testify to the many hours spent by her side in the kitchen. Long before I could reach the countertops, she would position me on a stool as her special little helper.

Now the kitchen felt empty. No songs of God's amazing grace filled the air. The room lacked the warmth of her joy and the light of her smile.

Flour, milk, brown sugar, apples, oats . . . I methodically checked off each ingredient. What was once a sacred time of communion had been reduced to a checklist. The sweet smell of vanilla—the scent I associate with being in her presence—filled the air. I longed for the days when I could wrap my arms around her flour-covered apron and lean into the fullness of her love.

Sounds of laughter rang out in the adjacent room as my family watched a game on TV. Before I could brace myself, my son ran into the kitchen and slammed into my thighs. "Mama, what you making?"

I scooped up a little bit of the mixture on a spoon and offered up a taste, just as my grandmother once did with me. The approval of a wide grin and tummy rub confirmed today's dessert would be a winner.

My grandmother's absence would be felt at this gathering, but she would be present in every smile, every laugh, and every sweet memory of home.

Father, in Your presence I find peace and hope. Thank You for those I love and who have loved me well. May their legacy of love lead me daily to invite others to taste and see that You are good.

—DR. SAUNDRA DALTON-SMITH

Catching Butterflies

What is your life? You are a mist that appears
for a little while and then vanishes.
—James 4:14 (NIV)

We drove for hours to spend the weekend with my parents during my dad's final weeks on earth. The trip was somber, although we did enjoy an enormous monarch butterfly migration as we passed through the state. During every rest stop, my husband, kids, and I giggled as we tried—unsuccessfully—to catch a butterfly.

We finally made it to my parents' house. Within a few hours, it became clear that my daddy no longer knew me. I showed him pictures, recalling our shared stories. "Look! It's me and you at my wedding. Remember?" But my dad's razor-sharp wit and unparalleled memory had faded. Disease had erased me from his mind.

Devastated, I took the kids to the park for fresh air. And wouldn't you know it? The butterflies followed us there, too. I smiled while my kids again unsuccessfully tried to capture a butterfly. Watching their adorable exasperation amid unspeakable beauty, I thought, *My loves, you don't need to hold them in your hand to appreciate them. Enjoy them as they are, even while they move away from you.* The scene replayed itself for me in the weeks that followed, as my dad faded into final rest, heaven bound.

I thanked my heavenly Father for a gracious illustration of His love from above. The Lord used a flood of monarchs to remind me: My time with my dad—all of our time on this earth—is fleeting. Certainly the presence of my dad's body on earth is not necessary for me to appreciate the gift of his life.

Lord, thank You for gently leading my broken heart into Your pastures of comfort. Thank You for the anticipation of a new heaven and new earth, where we dwell in Your presence forever.

—MOLLY DEFRANK

Paul

Do everything in love.
—1 Corinthians 16:14 (NIV)

Paul was the first student I lost.

As a student teacher in rural Kentucky, my head was stuffed full of classroom theory about how to be an English teacher. But it was actually the impact from Paul's death that forged me into the teacher I became.

He was the smallest boy in the ninth grade, lagging far behind friends who had already begun their growth spurt. He was an easy target for their practical jokes.

I arrived early each day, eager to impress my supervising teacher, but my ironic daily duty was to release Paul from the broom closet, where his roguish classmates had imprisoned him. Since there was no handle on the inside of the closet, he pounded on the door until freed.

Every morning as he walked out of the closet, sheepish grin on his face, brown eyes smiling at the joke, he mumbled a soft "Thank you" and ran off to join his comrades. It was a strange ritual, one never discussed in any college textbook I had ever read.

One spring morning, as bloodroot and Virginia bluebells blossomed under clear skies, Paul took out a small boat and fished on his family's pond. It was there, in the tranquility of a beautiful day, that a boating accident ended his life.

Years later, my heart still aches over Paul's senseless death, but it molded my philosophy of teaching. The jolt I received from losing Paul taught me something no classroom lecture ever would. I was reminded of the brevity of life and how important it is to display love to my students every single day.

Lord, help me to always treat my students and other people with respect, honor, and love because they are all Your precious children.

—LORI DURHAM

Golden Earrings

You shall come to your grave in ripe old age, as a shock of grain comes up to the threshing floor in its season.
—Job 5:26 (RSV)

As I held the gold sunburst earrings in the palm of my hand, I thought of the older woman who had worn them and left them to me in her will. Ginny was a dear friend of my mother's generation, and the age difference had, if anything, only made our bond of friendship stronger.

We were both childless widows who lived alone; after my mother died, Ginny seemed to slide naturally into a role as a second mother to me. God must have known how much I needed the love and comfort of an older woman. We sat together in church and ate lunch together afterward; we confided in each other about how much we missed our husbands and how many changes life had brought us. Ginny had an infectious, tinkling.

I had never been able to face the reality of Ginny's death, although she was so much older than I was. Now, holding the delicate earrings in my hand, I looked at the tiny sapphires in the center of the golden sunburst frame. Ginny knew that I, like her, had never pierced my ears. As I gently screwed the earrings onto my ears for the first time, I felt a deep ache inside, knowing I would never be able to hear her voice. But . . . when the earrings were firmly in place, I seemed to hear a very faint, tinkling laugh.

What Ginny had left me was far more than a pair of precious earrings. She had given me a clear reminder that deep friendship never dies. She would be with me always, and every time I wore these earrings, I would hear that faint tinkling laugh.

Lord, You know how much we miss those we love who have passed on to be with You in heaven. Please accept our deep gratitude for reminding us that their loving presence remains with us always.

—PEGGY EASTMAN

God Is Always with You

Do not be afraid, for I am with you. Do not be anxious,
for I am your God. I will fortify you, yes, I will help you.
—Isaiah 41:10 (NWT)

My friend Taylor's mom passed away unexpectedly. A couple of days before, Taylor had urged her mom to go to the doctor since she had not been feeling well. Her mom declined, thinking she just needed some rest.

While Taylor was at work, she realized her mom hadn't called—even after Taylor left voice and text messages. My friend decided to leave work and go to the home they shared. When she arrived, there were no signs that her mom had been up and about, and it was late afternoon. Sadly, she found her mom still in bed and no longer alive.

Taylor had no other living relatives and was filled with loneliness. She had never imagined life without her mother. I badly wanted to comfort Taylor, but it was understandably difficult to do so as she grieved. I tried to constantly reassure her that God was with her and would see her through this time. I prayed hard for Taylor, especially after she stopped taking my phone calls and withdrew from mutual friends.

A few weeks later, I got a call from Taylor asking if I would come over and watch movies. I was thrilled that she was attempting to bring normalcy back into her life. While she was in the kitchen making popcorn, I noticed Isaiah 41:10 printed out and taped to the front of her Bible. I immediately thanked God! This was the same scripture I had been meditating on as I prayed for my friend. God had heard and answered both our prayers.

God, please ease my grief and anxieties. Please remind me that
You are here to help me and offer hope when I can see no happiness
for my future. In Jesus's name, Amen.

—ADRIENNE FARR

Call Your Father

So in everything, do to others what you would
have them do to you . . .
—Matthew 7:12 (NIV)

Southwest Wyoming is wide, windswept, and sparsely populated. I was traveling in a rented minivan from Salt Lake City to Yellowstone National Park when I entered the small town of Kemmerer, Wyoming.

Why did that name sound so hauntingly familiar? Meandering through town, I soon spotted what I didn't even know I was looking for: J.C. Penney Store Number One, affectionately known as The Mother Store. Young James Cash Penney arrived in the sheep ranching and coal mining community of Kemmerer in 1902 to open a one-room general merchandise store known as The Golden Rule. From that inauspicious beginning, J.C. Penney grew to be one of the biggest retailers in the world.

I knew the story well because my dad was a Penney manager for more than thirty years. He instilled in me the lessons he'd learned and taken to heart: honesty, hard work, enthusiasm, thrift, attention to detail, and—most of all—treating others the way you want to be treated. The Golden Rule.

I was so thrilled I could hardly stand it. I was in the very town where J.C. Penney started! I pulled my cell phone from my purse. *Wait till Daddy hears this,* I thought. *And wait till he sees the pictures I'm going to send him.* Then it hit me. My father had gone to be with his heavenly Father more than twenty years ago. I couldn't call him on the phone. I couldn't send him any pictures.

But there was something I could do. I could wander in wonder up and down every aisle of the very first J.C. Penney store. I knew for certain that Daddy, with a great big grin on his face, was wandering them with me.

Heavenly Father, help me to take to heart the good lessons my earthly father taught me.

—JENNIE IVEY

More Than Once

For the wages of sin is death, but the gift of God is
eternal life in Christ Jesus our Lord.
—Romans 6:23 (NIV)

I entered the restaurant with a sigh. This is where my favorite uncle Richard and I ate each time I visited him. After his diagnosis of Stage IV larynx cancer I accompanied him to all his medical appointments because he had severe hearing problems.

One day I asked, "Are you going to go to heaven when you die?"

"I don't know," he replied.

"Jesus died to save you from your sins. All you have to do is believe in Him and ask His forgiveness for your sins and ask Him to come into your heart. He'll forgive you and take you to heaven when you die. Do you want to pray that prayer with me?"

"I suppose so," he said in his heavy Finnish accent. Then he repeated my words as I prayed a prayer for salvation.

Months later, I asked, "Now do you know you'll go to heaven after you die?"

He looked at me with wide eyes. "Do I have to say it more than once?"

I laughed. "No, you don't. You've asked God into your heart. He has forgiven you and will take you to heaven." He exhaled a deep relief and nodded.

Now I sat at a table alone, missing my uncle. Suddenly the woman at the next table with two unruly boys raised her voice, "Do I have to say it more than once? Now settle down!"

I laughed. Those words were a reminder that Richard was having a wonderful eternal life with Jesus, even though he only said it once.

Dear Heavenly Father, thank You for sending your Son to die so we may have a wonderful eternal life with You, and for forgiving our sins each day.

—CONNIE LOUNSBURY

Finding Beauty amid the Ashes

And provide for those who grieve in Zion—to bestow on
them a crown of beauty instead of ashes, the oil of joy
instead of mourning, and a garment of praise instead of
a spirit of despair. . . .
—Isaiah 61:3 (NIV)

Journal pages curled beneath my fingertips, the ink marred by tears. It was the first time I'd written out the story of my loss and grief. The words felt raw and gritty, laced with pain so acrid I could almost taste it.

The story seemed broken. Reading back over the words, I couldn't help but get the sense that "this was not supposed to happen." Huddled on my knees, I cried out to God: *Why God, why?*

The lightning bolt moment never came. All I heard were two simple words: *Trust Me.*

Clinging to His truth for dear life, I took my seemingly broken story and laid it before Him. There were no answers. I could only trust that the God of the universe held these curled and battered pages in His hands— that He could see where I could not.

And in the process of letting go, true beauty emerged. For in the grief falling onto Him, I found the ability to sing through the storm. What once looked broken was now a testament to His great faithfulness through it all. Trusting in Him, ashes gave way to grace.

As I redirected my eyes heavenward, He simultaneously changed the way I saw my story: beautiful in all its brokenness. As I trusted in Him alone, this bruised chapter found greater purpose.

Father God, it is only in You that our broken stories are redeemed and transformed. We thank You that even when there are no earthly answers, You are enough.

—LIZ MANNEGREN

Knowing Where to Start

Why, my soul, are you downcast? Why so disturbed within me? . . .
—Psalm 42:5 (NIV)

It had been years since I sat on the couch in my counselor's office, seeking Ms. Linda's professional help through postpartum depression. At least there had been a logical explanation that time, but now, the cause of my sadness could not be pinpointed so easily.

Was it the sudden loss of my brother-in-law? The shock of losing my job? Maybe it was worry for my family members who were drowning in grief. Or maybe it was just a bad case of the winter blues and I was overreacting.

All I knew was that I was at the end of myself. Nothing I did seemed to help. Praise songs couldn't lift my spirits. Reading Scripture didn't alleviate the pain. Not even prayer could dissipate the funky fog of despair that seemed closer to me than my own shadow.

"What's troubling you?" Ms. Linda prompted in a soothing voice.

I unfolded the paper I had prepared and stared at it in silence. "I don't even know where to begin," I finally said.

She tilted her head. "Why don't you start with what hurts most."

That simple suggestion was exactly what I needed to hear for God to begin the slow process of healing in my heart. Ms. Linda's words were like an angelic message straight to my soul, proclaiming God's invitation to cry into His arms, tell Him where it hurt, and relax as He held me through it.

Now, any time I cannot make sense of my sorrow, I always start by telling my Father what hurts most.

Father, sometimes it's hard for me to understand why I feel the way I do. Thank You for people of faith who help me wade through my emotions, and thank You for comforting me when I tell You what hurts most.

—EMILY E. RYAN

Promises to Keep

But as for you, be strong and do not give up,
for your work will be rewarded.
—2 Chronicles 15:7 (NIV)

After another failed attempt to concentrate, Mom placed a book on the table beside her recliner. "I promise to read it when I feel better."

We both knew the truth. The fight against cancer took all her energy. She would never read my first published novel.

Mom had encouraged my dream since childhood. She supplied postage so I could write pen pals, and celebrated my first publication at age nine, a poem in *Jack and Jill* magazine. But she could never read more than the first few pages of my book.

I made a promise to Mom as well. She would spend her final days at home. I moved in for several months and, with the help of hospice, kept my word. After Mom's funeral, exhaustion and grief settled in. Then my husband was diagnosed with leukemia. Another battle for life ensued. I had experienced too much real life with people I loved to make up stories about make-believe characters. I quit writing.

Many months later, while rummaging through an old box, I found a tattered book. "To open the heart and rekindle the spirit of writers" was printed beneath the title. I opened the cover. A note in familiar writing read, "Maybe this book will give you a little inspiration. Love, Mom," with the date Dec. 14, 2001. Printed on a bookmark tucked between the pages was a poem titled "Don't Quit."

I pressed the book to my heart. Mom had been gone nearly two years. But God knew I needed her encouragement—and His—preserved inside that long-forgotten gift I'd packed away many years ago.

Father, sometimes the plans You have for me are difficult to see.
Please give me the strength to fulfill Your purpose for my life.

—KAREN SARGENT

Family Tree

Where, O death, is your victory? Where, O death, is your sting?
—1 Corinthians 15:55 (NIV)

A headstone, carved in advance of death, seemed unsettling to me—name, birthdate, dash, and blank spot for the death date. A visit to a cemetery with Aunt Treva changed my view.

"I enjoy visiting the cemetery," Aunt Treva said. "I have more friends and family here than I do in town." At eighty-four, her playful statement contained truth.

From headstone to headstone, we shared memories from our family tree. The highlight of the day was discovering a headstone engraved with "Treva Buchholzer." Below the name was "1910," followed by a dash and a blank spot.

"Doesn't it feel strange to read your own headstone?" I asked.

"Not a bit," Aunt Treva replied. "You want to take a picture?" She plopped down on the marble base, crossed her legs, and flung one arm across the top of the headstone. Then she flashed a big smile, and I snapped a picture.

"Hey, do you want me to lie down so you'll know how I'm going to look?" she asked.

"Please don't!" I exclaimed. We belly laughed about death.

I treasure the day Aunt Treva and I spent in a cemetery. Though her headstone now reads "1910–2001," the picture on my desk displays her smiling face and thumbs-up. That smile reminds me of her faith in Jesus, which allowed her to face the reality of death with laughter. That thumbs-up assures me that she now resides in heaven, and that someday, we will belly laugh together again.

Thank You, Jesus, that I do not have to fear death. I praise You for the promise of eternal life, for me and for those I love.

—BECKY ALEXANDER

Forty Days

Moses was there with the LORD forty days and forty nights without eating bread or drinking water. And he wrote on the tablets the words of the covenant—the Ten Commandments.
—Exodus 34:28 (NIV)

Spring had sprung, but I still grieved. My best friend Dorothy had been gone a year, but no matter how I tried, I couldn't "get over it." On my fortieth birthday, I sat outside on my patio amid the signs of spring. I scanned tree branches, imagining Dot pointing out birds. She loved to announce their scientific names and always seemed to sense my mood—which at that moment was very sad.

Then a colorful bird alighted on a tree beside my patio chair. "You've got to be a sapsucker," I said as it drummed a branch. Dot would've known its Latin name. I hurried inside to grab the bird book, bumping against the gold-framed Ten Commandments hanging on my kitchen wall. I paused to admire the hand-drawn calligraphy. Then I laughed.

During a luncheon celebrating two March birthdays, my dear friend had unveiled a piece just like this. I'd gasped with delight—until she admitted the gift was meant for the acquaintance. Still, my friend noted my crestfallen look. Soon after, she'd gifted me with the beautiful rendering I now tried to keep from shattering on the floor.

Thankfully, the picture didn't fall. As I straightened the frame, each of God's commandments seemed to speak in an inaudible voice that sounded a lot like my friend's. I stood in awe, filled with an incredible warmth. When grief tried to keep me down, the Ten Commandments and a Sphyrapicus (sapsucker) helped brighten my day.

Father, when grief rises anew and plunges me into sorrow, let me stop resisting and feel my feelings. And when things my loved one cherished come into view, let me see them as proof of Love that lasts forever.

—LINDA S. CLARE

Acres of Hope

And now, here's what I'm going to do: I'm going to start all over again. I'm taking her back out into the wilderness where we had our first date, and I'll court her. I'll give her bouquets of roses. I'll turn Heartbreak Valley into Acres of Hope....
—Hosea 2:14–16 (MSG)

From that last moment in the hospital sharing a final goodbye with my great-grandmother until the long drive from the gravesite, I have not been alone. Friends and family have cocooned me in their love. Their words of comfort sheltered me from a truth I cannot comprehend; the woman who raised me as her own will no longer be a part of my life.

Now that time has passed, they have moved on, but I have not, my emotions stuck between the past and the present. She was my safe place, my place of refuge. I wrestle with the thought that I may never feel that level of security and comfort again.

As winter rolls into spring, the warmth of the sun and the beauty of the budding dogwoods court my senses. I stroll through the overgrown yard. The smell of honeysuckle greets me, and leaves rustle overhead. Once again I feel cocooned, sheltered, and comforted.

Looking out over the yard, I am reminded of God's ability to rain upon the dry places to bring forth flowers in their season. Acres of hope spread out before me to testify of His faithfulness. I remove my shoes and wiggle my toes into the thick green grass. A few months ago, this same spot was brown and covered in frost, similar to my broken heart. Seeing its transformation gives me hope that I, too, can be restored to a thriving place.

Father, rain down on the dry places of life. Mend the broken pieces and restore my soul. Guide me through this winter season until I can see the first signs of spring burst forth from within me.

—DR. SAUNDRA DALTON-SMITH

Connecting the Dots

Blessed be the God and Father of our Lord Jesus Christ,
the Father of mercies and God of all comfort,
who comforts us in all our affliction. . . .
—2 Corinthians 1:3–4 (ESV)

This won't be your last experience with grief," the therapist told me. She was technically right, but in the wake of losing my father, her statement stung. His death shattered me, and I couldn't imagine my world crashing down like this again. Not until she reminded me that future suffering of this magnitude is inevitable. My dad's passing introduced me to a kind of crippling sadness—one that will return as soon as the next loved one passes on. My internal response to her observation was something along the lines of "Sheesh, thanks a lot."

But I also heard hope in her voice, a hope that changed the meaning of her statement. She said the words gently and kindly, as if they were a conversational doorway to peace and comfort, beckoning me to walk through. Finally, she added, "This place, this grief, is another valley in your life story where the Lord will meet you. Meet Him there."

Her words connected the scattered dots of my grief, revealing a bigger, clearer picture. I stepped back to see the context of my loss. Of death. My hope, my purpose, my joy did not die with my beloved daddy. My heart is tethered to an everlasting God. He meets me in my sorrow. And He will continue to meet me in every dark place of this broken world—until the day He brings me home. And when I get there? What a glorious day that will be.

Lord, thank you for using your people to speak truth and comfort into my life when I feel flattened by loss. When I am tempted to despair, please continue to lift my eyes to You, the author and perfecter of our faith.

—MOLLY DEFRANK

Reflections in My Mirror

For now we see only a reflection as in a mirror;
then we shall see face to face. Now I know in part;
then I shall know fully, even as I am fully known.
—1 Corinthians 13:12 (NIV)

I startled awake. Confused. Shaking. Rapid breaths.

A dream? A dream. Dear God, let this be reality.

We were together. All four of us: my husband, John, daughter, Allison, son, Russell, and me. Laughing around the dinner table. Happy. Safe. An alternate reality. A snapshot of what could have been. *Why, Russell? Why did you leave us?*

Eight years after his suicide, I still have more questions than answers, and my spirit is starved for understanding. After he died, I searched online for clues. I discovered posts on social media he had hidden from us but had shared with friends when he was young. Many painted unflattering pictures of me. He had been angry at me, and I became convinced I was to blame for his death. It took months of counseling to understand I needed to let myself off the hook. When he died, Russell was twenty-seven. An adult. Old enough to make his own choices.

At the time he wrote those posts about me, he was a freshman in college. A naturally turbulent time as young adults begin to break free from parents' expectations and pave their own paths in life.

But still, in dreams, my troubled spirit conjures images of what could have been had we only been given a chance to help when he needed us most. For now, the mirror I hold in my hand only reflects my face. But one day, I will understand more fully. One day, we will be together again as a family, and not in a dream. Laughing around a table. And finally, really at home.

Lord, I long for the day when I can see clearly through the mirror.
Until then, ease my troubled spirit and help me accept my reality.

—LORI DURHAM

Message of the Mother Robin

And God is able to provide you with every blessing in
abundance, so that you may always have enough of everything
and may provide in abundance for every good work.
—2 Corinthians 9:8 (RSV)

As I passed my neighbor Richard's house while walking down our street, my steps slowed and I felt a mental nudge to go sit on his small front porch. Richard and I had often sat there talking about our neighborhood; he was the longtime volunteer chairman of our village council and my friend. Richard had gone into the hospital a few weeks before with a severe respiratory infection and died there suddenly. I was devastated.

As I sat on Richard's porch, the chair next to me seemed very, very empty. I wanted to talk to him about our tall trees and the many varieties of birds that made our trees their home. How could anyone possibly fill Richard's shoes?

I thought about what his loss would mean to all of us, and then suddenly I heard a chirping noise nearby. A robin was flying back and forth. I looked around the side of the house to see a nest close by in a tree and realized a mother robin was feeding her young. Back and forth she flew, patiently feeding her insistent, cheeping babies with their little beaks raised.

I smiled and then almost laughed out loud. I could almost hear Richard's chuckle next to me. Surely this was a heaven-sent sign from Richard that our village would be fine. I could almost hear him saying in that strong, confident voice, "Don't worry; everything is going to be all right." Just as the mother robin was caring diligently for her young, so someone would come along to care diligently for our neighborhood. Now I was sure of it.

Lord God, when unexpected circumstances leave us feeling bereft and worried about the future, You always find ways to comfort us and bring us hope.

—PEGGY EASTMAN

Mourning Kobe

For as he thinketh in his heart, so is he . . .
—Proverbs 23:7 (KJV)

Kobe Bryant just died in a helicopter crash!" My brother and I had been rapturous fans of his for almost twenty years and the panic in his voice was palpable. I flipped through various news outlets to see if this was true. Sadly, his death was a fact. Subsequently, it was confirmed that Kobe's 13-year-old daughter and seven others perished with him. I sobbed uncontrollably.

Seeing flashbacks of all the memorable games he played made my heart wrench. I cried often. As fans we feel such a connection to stars of sports or entertainment. They evoke feelings of joy and love for the way they perform. However, I truly had no idea such intense grief could come over someone I had never met. I was treating this horrible situation, though worthy of misery, as if it happened to a family member.

As the days wore on and my bereavement continued, I noticed how many people within my network were passing away. A friend watched her uncle die. A former coworker passed away. Another friend lost her brother. I felt as though my grieving was drawing this sorrowful news my way, and I had better shift my energy before I was the one reporting a loss.

I reached out to a good friend and asked if she knew of scriptures that could help. She sent many, but Proverbs 23:7 stood out. By meditating on this scripture, I allowed sad thoughts to pass through me and be replaced with joyous experiences. With the grace of God I was finally able to elevate out of the unexpected grief I felt.

Father, please uplift and bless all those dealing with loss. Please comfort and wrap them in Your arms. Please let them know You are here in their time of need.

—ADRIENNE FARR

Stronger Than Ever, Every Spring

*Consider how the wild flowers grow. They do not labor
or spin. Yet I tell you, not even Solomon in all
his splendor was dressed like one of these.*
—Luke 12:27 (NIV)

I head down the driveway to retrieve my mail and notice my neighbor going wild with weed spray. I wave and tell him good morning. "No matter how hard I try, I can't get rid of all this," he says with an exasperated sigh.

"Poison ivy?" I ask.

"Nope. These pesky wild violets. Seems like no matter how much I spray, they come back every spring stronger than ever."

I pulled the mail from the box and wished him luck. Then I went inside and took from a cabinet one of the juice glasses that had belonged to my mother. In springtime, the glasses became wildflower-filled vases that lined the windowsill above our kitchen sink. I ran water into the glass and headed back outside to pick a handful of wild violets to put in the jar.

Then I looked up toward heaven. "I got it, Mother," I say. "Our first bouquet."

What my neighbor thinks of as an annoyance reminds me of my mother. I can hear her telling me the old, old story of why violets are her favorite flower. "They're one of the first signs of spring," she says. But that's not the main reason she loves violets so. "God does all the work," she says. "He sends them back every year, stronger than ever. All we have to do is enjoy them."

My neighbor is still at it with his weed spray. Not me, though. I raise the glass of violets to my nose and inhale their sweet smell.

Thank You, God, for the wild violets of spring. And for a mother who loved them and passed her appreciation along to me.

—JENNIE IVEY

The Tree

*Let a little water, I pray you, be fetched, and
wash your feet, and rest yourselves under the tree.*
—Genesis 18:4 (KJV)

I unlocked the door of the apartment and stepped in.

The space was tiny. To my right a galley kitchen sported five feet of counters interrupted by a stove and sink. Ahead, the living room had space at the near end for a small table. I closed my eyes and told myself, *Just get through it, Wanda. You have to find a place.* In a month my house would be sold, and I had to move to town. I'd chosen to look at this apartment first because it had been built by a good friend when his family quit ranching.

I walked across the carpet to the long bank of windows and pulled open the drapes. The thick luxuriant branches of a stately blue spruce—its arms open in welcome—met my gaze. I gaped in astonishment. I love evergreens! And I have never had one, though I tried for years to grow them.

I stretched my neck out of the window to find the top. The tree rose all the way up to the roof of the two-story building. A bird feeder dangled midway. Sparrows shot away in alarm, chittering at me. Beneath the spruce, red scoria rocks lay scattered as mulch on the ground. Someone must have taken good care of this evergreen, because it had obviously thrived.

I felt a grip around my heart loosen, like a thin band of iron I'd not known was there, and peace entered in. That tree was a blessing, a promise from God that wherever I went, He would be beside me.

"Okay," I said. "I'll move here, Lord." Because the tree was a gift from Him, and I knew it.

Dear God, Your compassion still overwhelms me. How You love Your children. Thank You so much for giving me that desire of my heart. Amen.

—WANDA ROSSELAND

Feeling Better

Now may the Lord of peace himself give you peace at all times and in every way. The Lord be with all of you.
—2 Thessalonians 3:16 (NIV)

About a week after my mother's funeral, I developed a bad cold. My energy waned as I moped around sneezing and blowing my nose. In the kitchen, I poured myself yet another glass of orange juice. "That will make you feel better," my husband said.

That was what my mother always said when she handed me a glass of hot lemonade whenever I was sick. When she rubbed Vicks VapoRub on my chest, the strong smell always made my eyes water, but Mom said, "It will make you feel better."

Dave's words made me think about my mother. Had I done enough for her when she lived with us after her stroke? Did I take enough time to talk with her? Play cards with her? Take her places? She had been a good mother. Had I been a good enough daughter? I had been busy in my office writing so much of the time. Had she been lonely during those times?

I grabbed my heavy fleece throw and lay down for a nap plagued with regret for things I might have done. I awoke with a start. The smell of Vicks was strong in the room. As quickly as I sat up the smell dissipated. *Vicks? Mom? This will make you feel better.*

That message from heaven did make me feel better. I knew I had done the best I could for Mom. She understood the need for me to work part of each day, and she spent that time watching her favorite television shows. Thank You, Lord.

Dear Heavenly Father, thank You for Your Holy Spirit Who guides me and protects me and speaks to me in so many ways. I rejoice in Your love and I love You with all my heart.

—CONNIE LOUNSBURY

Travel-Sized Blessings

Your Father knows exactly what you need even before you ask him!
—Matthew 6:8 (NLT)

I walked into my friend's home for Bible study when a dozen voices cried in unison, "Surprise! Happy birthday!"

I was shocked. Half of the women in the group were new friends I'd only met a few weeks before. I never expected them to acknowledge, much less celebrate, my upcoming fortieth birthday, but somehow they planned an entire party without my knowing. After we enjoyed cake and discussed the week's lesson, they showered me with fun "forty-themed" gifts—forty pencils, forty pushpins, forty personalized Scripture cards. One friend even gave me forty travel-sized packages of tissues. We laughed as we imagined how long it would take me to use them all.

I was still giddy from my celebration when my husband called me on his way home the next evening. His voice sounded hollow. There had been an accident, he said. His brother had died in a plane crash a few hours earlier, and he had just found out.

I grabbed my first travel-sized tissue pack and cried into the folds. I was on my second pack the next morning when I had to tell our children their uncle was gone. By the weekend, on my actual fortieth birthday, I went through packages six and seven writing my brother-in-law's obituary.

While my friends and I had laughed at the idea of needing to buy tissues in bulk, God knew what a blessing they would soon become. By the time we said our final goodbyes at the cemetery a few days later, I had made a significant dent into the pile of tissue packages I thought I'd never need.

Heavenly Father, thank You for always knowing exactly what I need even before I do. You are providing before I ask and answering my prayers before I whisper them. Even in my grief, You are meeting my needs.

—EMILY E. RYAN

A Greater Love

I pray that you may . . . grasp how wide and long
and high and deep is the love of Christ.
—Ephesians 3:17–18 (NIV)

My husband, Matt, was shocked when he saw me stripping wallpaper off our kitchen wall.

"It's cheaper than therapy," I said. I was struggling with the grief of his mother's death, in addition to postpartum depression and the grayness of a Midwest winter.

Matt's mom loved others with a gentle extravagance. Though she was my mother-in-law, she was also my mentor. My heart ached on days I missed her the most. I longed to give back to her the love she had given me.

I thought a kitchen makeover would cheer me up. But after painting the walls a bright yellow, my grief and depression lingered. I asked God, "Why did You let me love someone so much that when she died, it hurts this bad?"

He responded with words I'll never forget. "As much as you loved Marie, I love you more."

I couldn't grasp the fact that God's love was greater than mine for Marie. Yet, in that moment, I felt deeply loved. Then I heard God whisper something else. "As much as you loved her, I, too, want your love."

That conversation was a turning point in my grief. New paint was a temporary fix for a wound left by loving and being loved so well. I was challenged to pursue a love that didn't end in death. Instead, God's love reached even deeper, showing me how human love is a reflection of the Almighty's never-ending affection.

Father, thank You for a love that's deeper and greater than any human love. As much as we miss our loved ones, equip us to return even a greater love to You. Amen.

—BRENDA L. YODER

Cody's Smile

My help comes from the LORD,
the Maker of heaven and earth.
—Psalm 121:2 (NIV)

A senior prom picture perfectly captured my friend's son, Cody—black tux, striking smile, strong and healthy, dashingly handsome.

One year later, Cody noticed a small bump on the left side of his neck.

The bump grew quickly, and a radical surgery removed his left jugular vein, the muscle in his left shoulder, the nerve to his left vocal cord, a nerve to his bottom lip, and all of the lymph nodes in his neck. The cancer was relentless, and, in time, also attacked his intestines and one hip.

The last time I saw Cody, he barely possessed the strength to sit in a wheelchair. He was almost unrecognizable at ninety-five pounds. But I did recognize him, because of his smile, though it now drooped on the left side.

Three years after the prom, Cody departed this earth. His unwavering faith in Jesus assured his family of his new home in heaven. Yet Angie missed her son desperately. On one especially hard day, she whispered a prayer: *"Jesus, help me. Please, help me."*

In an instant, Cody's smiling face appeared. "I'm okay!" he said.

She opened her eyes, and he was gone.

Angie holds tightly to the two-word message of hope she received that day. The ache of separation from Cody still floods her heart often. When it does, she closes her eyes and pictures his blond hair, green eyes, deep dimples, and heavenly smile.

Dear Jesus, this separation from the ones we love causes great pain in my heart. We lift up our eyes to You. Thank You for help and comfort—for today, for tomorrow, and for all of the hard days ahead.

—BECKY ALEXANDER

Circle of Light

The light shines in the darkness, and
the darkness has not overcome it.
—John 1:5 (NIV)

A few days after my sister-in-law passed away from colon cancer, I sat at the kitchen table and tried to read my Bible for reassurance. I say tried to read—outside, rain slapped against the window and the lights flickered with each wind gust. More importantly, losing Connie made my spirit ache. When her family had lived with us for three months, we held impromptu Bible studies and sang hymns as we folded laundry.

I was re-reading chapter one in John's gospel when the power went out. While my husband looked for a flashlight, I sat in the dark and thought of his sister. Connie's deep brown eyes, her precise way of folding a T-shirt, her infectious laugh—all these things brightened my mood for a moment before fading away. I sighed. I would miss my wonderful sis-in-law.

My husband came back wielding one of his many flashlights and saw me with my head in my hands. "I can't believe it, either," he said and patted my back. "Connie and I went through so much together. The year we lived in the San Diego Mission after Mom's car crash, we vowed to always be there for each other."

I looked up at him. "I'm so sad. How will we go on without her?"

"I haven't told you about my dream." He pointed the flashlight at the open Bible. "Connie came to me and said, 'No matter what happens, stay in the circle of light.'"

As we marveled about how near Connie felt, the house lights switched back on.

Lord, losing my loved one leaves a hole in my heart. Yet when I receive a reassuring sign, I know that both You and my loved one are closer than ever. Thank You for the comfort that comes when You shine a little light on the darkness.

—LINDA S. CLARE

Selah Moments

Trust in Him at all times, you people; Pour out your heart before Him; God is a refuge for us. Selah.
—Psalm 62:8 (NKJV)

The deep reverberating sound of the organ filled the sanctuary as the first chords played. A sound I normally love but was currently unable to enjoy. It reminded me of the pain attached to loving.

The building chorus ascended higher and higher until at last it reached a crescendo. My life had followed a similar pattern, building testimony upon testimony and moving from glory to glory until it reached a crescendo.

These crescendo moments are extended moments of stress. They stretched me beyond my faith comfort level and required a deeper level of trust. They caused me to pay attention because what happened would determine the song I sang.

In an attempt to avoid the pain of loss, I withdrew from anything I could potentially lose in the future. I reasoned if I didn't hold on to anything too tight, it wouldn't hurt so bad if it slipped out of my grasp. In the process, I lost my song.

It was in the tension of the crescendo that I realized I was most in need of a moment to pause and listen. A *selah* moment to stop the noise long enough hear what the next verse holds.

During each selah, I am invited to reflect on what has been and what is yet to come. It is the moments after every prayer when I stop giving God my requests and instead leave space for Him to answer.

Each *selah* moment is a reprieve from striving, an opportunity to pour out and be filled. Each is a time to be quiet before God, while He sings over me.

Father, You are my safe place. You are my comfort during times of stress, my peace when I hunger for rest. Give me ears to hear the sound of the song You are singing over me.

—DR. SAUNDRA DALTON-SMITH

Grief Doula

*He who dwells in the shelter of the Most High will abide
in the shadow of the Almighty.*
—Psalm 91:1 (NASB)

Losing my father brought deep pain, so I kept wishing it away. And wishing away pain reminded me of giving birth.

As any mom knows, the final stages of pregnancy can be brutal. One's body feels stretched beyond capacity. Everything hurts. By the time I reached my final weeks of pregnancy, I was ready to be finished. The transition from inside the womb to outside is life-altering. Because of this difficult process, many mothers have hired doulas to help them deliver their babies. A doula is like a coach and provides emotional support and help during delivery.

After my dad passed away, I kept coming back to doulas. I'd think, "The pain is too much. Is there someone who can help me? I need a grief doula!" If only there was some kind of help available to me outside myself . . . someone who could see the bigger picture, provide peace and strength as I navigated these waters.

Like a gentle tap on my shoulder, the names of God came to my mind. Jehovah Rapha: *Healer, the Lord Who Heals You*; Jehovah Shalom: *The Lord Is Peace*; Jehovah Nissi: *The Lord Is My Banner*; Jehovah Jireh: *The Lord Will Provide*; El Roi: *The God Who Sees*; El Shaddai: *God Almighty*.

There I was, looking to invent a new kind of doula. All along, the Lord of Peace, the God Who sees, the God Almighty, Father—had already sent His very Spirit to be with me in my grief.

Lord, thank You that Your very names testify to Your tender care for me. Please remind me in my pain and sadness that you see me, and you offer me peace that surpasses understanding.

—MOLLY DEFRANK

Perfect Imperfections

And we know that in all things God works for the good of those who love him, who have been called according to his purpose.
—Romans 8:28 (NIV)

I stepped back to examine my front door with a critical eye. The first coat of paint had already dried, but some primer was still visible. I definitely needed a second coat to cover the imperfections.

And then I thought, *You've already wasted too much time trying to cover the imperfections of life.* My son's death had shattered me. Because I felt stigmatized by the taboo of Russell's suicide, I had not been honest with friends and family. It was easier to pretend he had died accidentally than to reveal the ugly truth.

This duplicity came at a cost. I was torn into fragments trying to figure out which ones I could openly talk with without receiving judgment. I worried what others would think about me. About Russell. About some flaw in our family's dynamics. The rabbit holes of my mind looped endlessly.

Eventually I grew exhausted painting over the inconvenient truth, and I began to accept my life's story. I resolved that, for God to use me to help others, I had to become transparent with them.

At first it was easiest to do this with the high school students I taught. They listened sympathetically to my story. Some even told me they needed help, so I provided resources to assist them. I kept a vigilant watch over my students, looking for signs of depression and anxiety so I could intervene when necessary. I worked closely with the school's guidance department. Over time, I began to openly reveal my story because I discovered that it's our imperfections that actually enhance the durability of our lives and bind us all together.

Lord, give me the courage to use the imperfections of my own life to help others around me who are hurting and broken.

—LORI DURHAM

Judging Jester

The LORD does not look at the things people look at.
People look at the outward appearance,
but the LORD looks at the heart.
—1 Samuel 16:7 (NIV)

My friend Nala and I were reminiscing. "Jester was crazy!" she said. The three of us went to high school together and every hilarious story we recounted involved Jester's antics. "It's a shame he turned to drugs," I said. "Do you know where he is now?" Nala said she was still in very close contact with Jester's sister. Now a father of three, Jester had lung cancer.

A few months later, Nala told me, "Jester passed away yesterday." I felt deep pangs in my stomach at hearing this news and grieved for his children. "That's horrible," I sobbed. "Now he's gone and he didn't even give himself the chance to make things right with God." Nala looked at me inquisitively. "How do you know he hasn't made things right with God?"

In that moment I realized how I'd judged Jester for as long as I'd known him. I distanced myself from him, thinking he wasn't good enough to befriend. I didn't answer his calls, even though he could've been reaching out for help. I remembered feeling sorry for his mom, a consistent church-goer, when I found out he was an addict. I thought how humiliated she must feel having a son that wouldn't reunite with loved ones in the afterlife.

Nala woke me from my thoughts. She had been looking through her phone and began reading 1 Samuel 16:7. I hadn't recognized how much judgment I exhibited, or how easy it was to fall into judging someone. "Let God be the judge," she said. I agreed. I would pray for Jester and for his grieving family and strive to see the good in everyone.

Father, please give us the strength to recognize when we are standing in judgment of others and bless us with the will to seek out scriptures to help enlighten those around us.

—ADRIENNE FARR

Don't Get Stuck with the Old Maid!

Our mouths were filled with laughter,
our tongues with songs of joy. . . .
—Psalm 126:2 (NIV)

Nobody's house was more fun to visit than Great-Aunt Sybil's. She lived near a swamp in Florida, where alligators sometimes crawled onto the bank to bask in the sun. She had a drawer in her kitchen filled with sweet treats. Best of all, she always had a deck of Old Maid cards shuffled and waiting in the middle of the round glass table in her sunroom.

Aunt Sybil didn't follow the rules. No pretending she didn't have the Old Maid when she did. No trying to disguise her delight when it was drawn from her hand. No acting like she wasn't overjoyed when someone else was left holding the Old Maid when the game ended. My siblings and I always had laughter-induced stomachaches after playing cards with Aunt Sybil.

I was eleven when Aunt Sybil died. Heartbroken, I vowed I'd never play Old Maid again. It would be too sad without her. Decades passed and I kept my word. But then I had grandchildren. Grandchildren who came to visit one weekend bearing a deck of Old Maid cards and begging me to play. Know what? I said yes. I offered treats from my own yum-yum drawer. I told the kids all about Aunt Sybil. Now, whenever they visit, we play Old Maid. I make it obvious when I'm holding the accursed card. I'm delighted when it's drawn from my hand. I whoop and holler when someone else is stuck with the Old Maid when the game ends. My grandchildren laugh until their stomachs hurt.

So do I. And so does Aunt Sybil, who I'm certain is looking down on us and enjoying every minute. I'm only sorry it took so long to figure out she'd never really left me.

Thank You, Lord, for laughter and for loved ones, abiding now with You, who taught us to find joy in the simple things.

—JENNIE IVEY

Frannie

*But he said to me, "My grace is sufficient for you,
for my power is made perfect in weakness." Therefore,
I will boast all the more gladly about my weaknesses,
so that Christ's power may rest on me.*
—2 Corinthians 12:9 (NIV)

I hadn't seen my sister-in-law Frannie since I divorced her brother—even though I loved and missed her. "Call me. I love you," she had said the last time I saw her. But I didn't call her. I rejoiced at the announcement of her new marriage but only sent a card with an excuse for not attending. I meant to stay in touch but didn't. Was it guilt? Was it fear of judgment? I don't know.

She was on my mind so much that I finally made the call after almost a year since her remarriage. Her husband, whom I had never met, answered. "It grieves me to tell you Frannie passed away about a month ago."

I couldn't speak. Frannie. Gone. Buried. Why hadn't I called her sooner? She must have felt so betrayed when I dropped our friendship. Her words echoed in my head: *Call me. I love you.* She counted me as a friend regardless of whether I was married to her brother. She had left it up to me to take the first step.

I realized I was pacing. Was "Ave Maria" sung at her funeral like she wanted? Did she wear the blue dress I had promised to make sure she wore? I had let her down. *Forgive me, Frannie. God, forgive me,* I prayed.

Unable to focus on anything, I turned on the television that was set to my music station. "Ave Maria" was playing. My prayer had been heard and answered. I was forgiven.

Thank You, heavenly Father, for Your love, Your grace, and Your forgiveness, none of which I deserve. Please help me to be a better person and to think more about others.

—CONNIE LOUNSBURY

A Time to Dance

You have turned my mourning into joyful dancing.
—Psalm 30:11 (NIV)

Afew years after my mother died, I asked my dad why he never took us to the cemetery to visit her grave. I'd seen families do this in the movies. Why didn't we?

"Because she's not there," he said pragmatically. "Her body may be, but why go to a cemetery to mourn when her soul is in heaven?" His logic made sense, and I easily followed suit as an adult, only visiting her grave on a handful of special occasions.

It wasn't until my daughter Adelle had her first dance recital that things changed. The recital venue was across the street from the cemetery, and on dress rehearsal day, I couldn't resist an impromptu visit.

Adelle tiptoed around the headstones in her ballet shoes, the sunlight bouncing off the glitter in her tutu, and paused respectfully when I pointed out Mom's grave. "She would have loved seeing you in your costume," I said, silently wondering if eternity's windows ever allowed such moments. "Did you know she used to dance too?"

Adelle's eyes grew wide as I told her of endless hours at the dance studio, rehearsals for *The Nutcracker*, and mom's pointe shoes which I still had in the attic. Adelle danced into an arabesque and posed while I took photos.

The visit turned into a cherished annual tradition. After dress rehearsals, we'd drive across the street, where Adelle would share her costumes and ballet routines with the grandmother she never had a chance to meet in person. Three generations of women enjoying a springtime afternoon of ballet. Dad had been right. Why go to a cemetery to mourn when you can go to dance?

Thank You, God, for turning my tears into smiles in a way that only You can. In my times of mourning and times of dancing, help me to remember that You are equally faithful in both.

—EMILY E. RYAN

Divine Calling

And the God of all grace, who called you to His eternal glory in Christ, after you have suffered a little while, will Himself restore you and make you strong, firm and steadfast.
—1 Peter 5:10 (NIV)

After twenty-nine years pastoring a country church, my father-in-law, Bill, gave up the pulpit. Ministrokes had taken away his ability to comprehend scripture or study books by spiritual leaders. Even reading the newspaper was a struggle.

A neurologist explained that small blood vessels in his brain were collapsing, causing the episodes. After each episode, Bill would experience various effects. At times, his speech would be slurred or movement in his right hand impaired. He might confuse the telephone with the remote control or forget how to tell time on the clock.

Eventually, Bill napped most of the day and rarely left home except Sunday mornings, and he no longer attended evening services.

One afternoon Bill sat in his recliner while his wife prepared dinner. His voice carried into the kitchen, clearer and stronger than it had been in months. At first, she thought he was talking to her. Then she realized she was overhearing a one-sided conversation, as if eavesdropping on a telephone call. She sensed a holy presence. Bill was engaged in a divine conversation—with whom? Jesus? An angel? The only words she understood clearly were "Yes, I'm ready."

During dinner Bill repeated the words to her, "I'm ready." She didn't mention the private conversation she heard. She simply assured him she would be okay. Bill went to bed early that evening and woke up in eternity.

Father, thank You for preparing an eternal place for us with You, for saving us from the suffering on earth, and for making all things new.

—KAREN SARGENT

Bathed in Mystery

I have set my rainbow in the clouds, and it will be
the sign of the covenant between me and the earth.
—Genesis 9:13 (NIV)

I stood on a chilly precipice at the Oregon coast. I held the urn containing my friend's ashes, hugging them close before her son scattered them over the Pacific Ocean. I didn't want to let her go. I silently pleaded for a sign that my wonderful friend was finally at rest. She was a bit older than my mother, but as close as a sister. I loved the way she rejoiced in God's mysteries. We wrote two books together, spent hours traveling to writing conferences, and confided in one another. She made it to age eighty-eight, and then she was gone.

As the winds carried her ashes away, waves crashed and seafoam covered the churning waters. I recalled her telling me about an evening when, recovering from a serious health scare, she'd soaked in her bathtub, meditating with candles around its edge. When she pulled the plug, she gazed at the swirling vortex around the drain. Then she'd smiled and exclaimed, "Hello, God!"

I stared at the waves, longing to see another swirling vortex, but the ocean was chaos, the sky a lifeless gray. Then as I squinted against the overcast, I saw a partial rainbow hanging in the mist. It reassured me that we'll meet again and that love eases the pain of loss.

As I walked away from the cliff, I glanced back. The rainbow now shimmered from horizon to horizon. "Hello, friend," I whispered. "Hello, God."

Lord, a pillar of cloud, a rainbow or even water swirling down a
drain comforts me when grief threatens to swallow me. Be comfort
in my sorrow; help me see Your love in both rainbow and stormy sea.

—LINDA S. CLARE

Unrelenting Fruit

They will be like a tree planted by the water that sends out its roots by the stream. It does not fear when heat comes; its leaves are always green. It has no worries in a year of drought and never fails to bear fruit.
—Jeremiah 17:8 (NIV)

When the first phone call went to voice mail, I refused to panic. It was only one missed call. But when the next ten calls also went unanswered, I knew something was wrong.

Bile rose in my throat when I heard the details of my nephew's suicide. I could feel my world start to tilt.

For weeks, I withdrew from God. I did not want to hear about His love or His faithfulness. Every word said in comfort ground against an open wound.

At times in life it seems the dry season will never end, when the rain fails to fall, and the refreshing streams seem miles away. Maybe this is why my grief led me to extended prayer walks.

On one humid summer day, I ventured out for a brief walk. Two hours later I was still walking. Given the unplanned circumstances, I soon realized I was in need of water. My failure to plan did not stop God's ability to provide.

Along the walking trail stood an apple tree, its limbs heavy with the weight of its fruit and a collection of ripe fruit around the base of the trunk.

The first bite was both tart and sweet. The juices from the apple mixed with my tears, each bite reminding me that even in a year of drought, God never fails to provide good fruit.

Father, Your love is unrelenting. It meets me in my desperation, guides me back to the still waters, and invites me to rest in You. Thank You for your lovingkindness toward me.

—DR. SAUNDRA DALTON-SMITH

Homecoming

"Bring the fattened calf and kill it. Let's have a feast and celebrate. For this son of mine was dead and is alive again; he was lost and is found." So they began to celebrate.
—Luke 15:23–24 (NIV)

During the height of WWI, my grandfather's family received a dreaded message from the War Department. He was missing in action, presumed dead.

But at war's end, he miraculously returned home. He described for his stunned family how he had hidden, severely injured, in a crater until discovered by some German soldiers. He pointed a pistol at them and ordered them to carry him to the nearest Red Cross station. To his surprise, the Germans did so, and my grandfather survived.

For several months after the death of my son, Russell, I expected to hear the front door open and see him walk once more into the house. I wouldn't have cared why he had disappeared. I would have only rejoiced to see him—just as my grandfather's family must have celebrated his return.

The process of letting go of the hope of seeing Russell at home once more has been the most difficult part of the grief experience for me. Accepting the finality of his death and realizing he wouldn't miraculously return home as my grandfather did has been a daily reality, difficult to face.

With each passing day, I have accepted a little bit more the melancholy truth that this reunion will not happen here on earth. At the same time, I anticipate the immense joy I will experience when I am once more able to wrap my arms around my son, who is only lost here on earth but is very much alive and safely at home with our heavenly Father.

Lord, thank You for the hope that comes through Your promises of life everlasting and the reunion of Your saints in glory.

—LORI DURHAM

I Heard the Voice

To everything there is a season, a time for every purpose
under heaven. A time to be born, and a time to die. . . .
—Ecclesiastes 3:1–2 (NKJV)

My friend Paula has never thought of herself as religious. Yet she knows without a doubt there's a heaven and that her mother, Ramona, is there.

Ramona developed a pulmonary embolism. Paula rushed to the hospital as soon as she got the news. "You're going to get well, Mom," she said.

"No, I'm not," Ramona answered. "I'm dying. I heard a voice that said it's time to go. It came straight from my heart."

Paula arranged for hospice care and moved Ramona home, where she lay in a hospital bed in the living room while her children and grandchildren came to say goodbye. Late on the evening of July Fourth, Paula sat alone by Ramona's bed. She turned up the volume on her cell phone and played one John Phillip Sousa march after another. "Mom was unconscious," Paula said, "but I reminded her how we used to play them together on the piano."

Ramona didn't indicate she'd heard. Overcome with emotion, Paula retreated to her mom's bedroom, collapsed into an armchair, and began thumbing through an old *Reader's Digest*. "As I read, the lamp started flickering," she said. "I knew without a doubt Mom was gone."

Paula still tears up when she tells the story of her mother's death. "I miss her something terrible," she says. "But I know for certain Mom's in heaven, and that I'll see her again someday."

Thank You, Lord, for the certainty of eternal life for those who
believe.

—JENNIE IVEY

Donna's Eyes

You have searched me, LORD, and you know me. You know when I sit and when I rise; you perceive my thoughts from afar.
—Psalm 139:1–2 (NIV)

It happened all at once. I got divorced, moved, and learned that my sister Donna's cancer had come back and she needed me to help her. Without a job, I took temporary office work to make ends meet and spent all my off hours with Donna.

After she died, I saw her eyes every time I looked in a mirror. Listless, sad eyes. I began to avoid looking at mirrors. It made me miss her more.

As months passed, I worked in several different offices. Then I got an evening temp job at a dance studio. I love to dance. Before long I was tapping my feet and smiling. But how could I be happy when my sister was dead?

One evening I entered the elevator with one of the dance instructors, and she made a comment. I laughed. Just then I turned and glimpsed my face in the mirrored wall. Donna's eyes were laughing! It shocked me so much I stopped laughing immediately. But I thought about those laughing eyes all evening. I remembered all the silly things we had done together before she died, and how much we had laughed together.

That night as I washed my face, I looked in the mirror and saw only my eyes. I realized I had turned a corner on my grief. God had shown me that Donna was laughing again. She was free of pain and was happy.

I still missed my sister, but I felt free to be happy again. I knew she had accepted Christ into her heart, and I'd see her again in heaven.

Thank You, heavenly Father, for sending Your son Jesus to die on the cross to save us from our sins so we can be forgiven and live in heaven with no pain or suffering forever.

—CONNIE LOUNSBURY

Elevator Messenger

*We can comfort those in any trouble with the comfort
we ourselves receive from God.*
—2 Corinthians 1:4 (NIV)

I fretted the entire two-hour drive to the hospital to see my husband. After a six-month battle with leukemia, he was scheduled for a bone marrow transplant. Our twenty-three-year-old daughter was his donor.

When I arrived at the hospital, the cancer center parking garage was closed, so I circled to the top level and parked. Loaded down with necessities for his month-long stay, I hauled myself to the elevators.

The elevator on the right was full. As the door closed, the left elevator opened, carrying only one passenger. The man inside scooted aside to make room for me. "You doing okay?" he asked.

I made a face. "A little crazy today."

"Me too. I come here every three months for labs and to see my doctor."

Every three months? Labs? Doctor? The routine sounded familiar like the one my husband would have if the transplant was successful. "May I ask why?"

"I had a bone marrow transplant seven years ago."

He looked strong, healthy. Suddenly, my load felt lighter. "My husband is having a transplant tomorrow." We stepped off the elevator, and I relayed my concerns. He shared his success story and assured me we'd have one too.

"Meeting you was a God thing," I said.

He agreed. "I never talk to people on elevators, but I knew I was supposed to talk to you." When I was surrounded by fear, God surrounded me with assurance by placing me in an elevator with a man who had survived the same battle my husband faced.

Father, the hard things in life equip me with understanding and compassion. May I comfort others the same way You comfort me.

—KAREN SARGENT

Jesus Loves Me

Sing to him, sing praise to him; tell of all his wonderful acts.
—1 Chronicles 16:9 (NIV)

I answered the phone tentatively. "Hi, Grams," I said. Since her recent stroke, my grandmother could no longer speak. My heart was broken in a million pieces. "How are things in Arizona?" Grams had been an elementary school music teacher, and she passed along her love of music to me. But now, the only sounds she made sounded like a lamb's bleat.

On the other end of the line, her wordless bleats were the only clue that she was still there. Maybe it was best if I kept talking. "The kids all miss you and so do I," I ventured. All four of my children, including my preschool-aged twins, lined up to each say, "I love you, GG." I told my grandmother the latest about our family and life in rainy Oregon. But as I ran out of news to share, the extended pause felt awkward.

Then my grandmother began to hum a tune I recognized. I put the phone on speaker and the kids sang out, "Jesus Loves Me!" Grams couldn't sing words, but she could still make music. I laughed and cried all at once.

Days later, Grams died from complications of her stroke, at age 89. At her service, aunts, uncles, cousins, and friends shared memories and then sat down to enjoy a meal in her honor.

At the table, my twin three-year-olds fidgeted and giggled. I whispered to them to be quiet, that we were there for GG. "You remember GG?" They looked at each other and then burst into song. "Jesus loves me, this I know." We adults laughed-cried. Grams might be singing with the angels, but through children's eyes, my grandmother was never far away.

Lord, it's so hard to lose someone you love. When sorrow sits on my chest like a ten-ton weight, lighten my grief with a song. Give me a song to sing to you. And when I can't cry another tear, help me remember to laugh.

—LINDA S. CLARE

The Meaning of a Rose

The wilderness and the solitary place shall be glad for them;
and the desert shall rejoice, and blossom as the rose.
—Isaiah 35:1 (KJV)

Mother's Day has always been a difficult Sunday for me. Each year I dread its approach because I know it will only serve as a reminder of loss and pain. A loss symbolized by a single white rose.

My mom's heavenly transition came hours after my birth. I never heard her laugh or saw her smile. We had no mother-daughter talks over milk and cookies. She wasn't there on my wedding day to fix my hair or hold my hand.

One memory I held from childhood Mother's Days happened every year at church. With envy, I watched as other kids filed into the sanctuary and received red roses to present to their moms at the appointed time in the church service. Each year, my heart twisting into knots, I received a white rose to commemorate my deceased mother.

Now that I have grown into a woman and became a mother myself, I am still moved by this ceremony of the rose. My heart rejoices over my children as they present their red roses to me. These days, I also choose to receive the single white rose in remembrance of my mom.

I choose to remember that a mother's love does not cease with death. I choose to find comfort in knowing we are healed and whole with Jesus. I choose to let my faith bloom like the rose.

Lord, You are faithfulness. You are a mother to the motherless and a father to the fatherless. You surround me with Your love. You shine the light of Your mercy upon me with each new day. You cause me to flourish in the place You have planted me. Help me to surrender to the process of healing the wounded pieces of my heart and learning to trust You more.

—DR. SAUNDRA DALTON-SMITH

A Wink from God

And surely I am with you always, to the very end of the age.
—Matthew 28:20 (NIV)

In middle school, our daughter, Allison, told us she'd seen the number 108 around her. A lot. Everywhere. Somewhat skeptical, we nonetheless started looking ourselves. To my great surprise, over the next several years, I also spotted the number all around me.

Most of the time, 108 seemed like a wink, a sign from God affirming He was with us. One day as I cleaned out a tub of discarded items, I spotted the parking decal I had used while pregnant with Allison. The number on the decal? 108. Another time, as we considered adopting a kitten, we were told the last three digits on her chip were 108. We took her straight home.

The morning of the memorial service for our son, Russell, was the hardest day of my life. I felt lost and alone even though I was surrounded by others. And still, after the service as many words of encouragement were offered to me, I felt the void of shock in my numbed spirit. I couldn't help but wonder where God was as emptiness consumed me.

On the way home from the service, we drove beside a broken-down school bus. I hardly gave it a glance except to think about the poor bus driver who still had to get his kids safely home. But then, my eyes landed on the big, black numbers painted on the side of the bus: 108.

Warmth crept into my broken heart. God had just given me a great big wink, affirming He was with me, even if I couldn't clearly see Him in the midst of my grief and pain.

Lord, Your ways are a mystery to me, but I thank You for sending signs to the brokenhearted reminding us that You are with us always, even to the end of the earth.

—LORI DURHAM

Right Here Beside Me

But when you pray, go into your room and shut the door. . . .
—Matthew 6:6 (RSV)

Today is Sunday and I'm home alone. That's not usually the case on the Sabbath. Attending Sunday school and worship service is one of the highlights of my week, and I hate to miss. But I've come down with a vicious cold I don't want to pass on to anyone else, so I'm watching church on YouTube.

My pastor welcomes everyone—in person and streaming—and makes announcements. There's the passing of the peace and then the organist chimes the hour—eleven bells. The choir processes to the front of the sanctuary, and the congregation joins in singing "Lift High the Cross."

I'm missing my great-grandmother something fierce this morning.

Her name was Jennie. Not coincidentally, that's my name, too. She lived with my family when I was a child and died when I was in seventh grade. Yet more than fifty years later, I remember Sunday mornings with her in vivid detail. Grandma was too frail to attend worship services with the rest of the family. But that didn't mean she didn't go to church. Every Sunday morning, she put on her nicest dress, twisted her hair into a neat bun, and dabbed on just a smidge of pale pink lipstick. Then she chose which gospel albums she wanted me to stack onto the record changer on her hi-fi stereo. With her Bible in her lap, Grandma would settle into her rocking chair.

"I wish you didn't have to be alone this morning," I would tell her.

Her answer was always the same. "Oh, honey, I'm not alone. Jesus is right here beside me." Now, as I sit in my own rocking chair on a quiet Sunday morning and watch church on my cell phone, I'm not alone, either. Jesus is right beside me.

So is Grandma.

For the saints who've gone before us, I'm grateful.

—JENNIE IVEY

The Word of the Year

Weeping may endure for a night, but joy cometh in the morning.
—Psalm 30:5 (KJV)

I never knew there was such a thing as "a word for the year" until I was sixty years old, so when God told me to do one after my husband Milton passed away, I immediately started arguing.

"Listen, God." I said. "I won't remember it past two weeks, and I really don't need another thing to keep track of."

He said, "It's *joy*." I felt like I'd been slugged in the stomach.

Mourning, grief, sorrow. Plenty of them. Tears, depression, heartbreak. Old friends. But joy? That had disappeared somewhere in the mists of yesterday.

I surrendered.

Quietly, joy began to peek out. At first, just the word, popping up to wave a flag like a little girl in a parade. I would open a book and there would be joy. Once I found the word in three consecutive paragraphs. I began to mark them with pink ink. I encountered signs on stores, picture frames, necklaces, rings, towels, cups. I started to think joy was waylaying me.

Six months after I was forced to begin this troublesome experiment, I felt like listening to some tunes. Paging through my dusty stack of CD's, my hand stopped on Elvis's *Moody Blue*. Within minutes, I was singing and dancing around the living room to "If You Love Me."

No doubt I was changing. Inside. And I was thinking. The thing is— Milton is always smiling in heaven. Whenever I imagine him up there, wondering what he is doing, his face is full of joy. And maybe that was what God wanted me to see, to learn. There is still happiness in the world, and if I look closely, a little joy.

Dear Lord, thank You for forcing me to find joy and for showing me happiness and a light heart again.

—WANDA ROSSELAND

A Song for Father

*The . . . Spirit you received brought about your adoption
to sonship. And by him we cry, "Abba, Father."*
—Romans 8:15 (NIV)

My half-sister, Kay, and I hugged in the hospital parking lot. "Now whatever we do," I said, "no crying. Dad won't want us to cry." Arm in arm, we arrived at the room where Dad—her father and my adopted father—lay dying.

He'd become a shadow of himself—former college football quarterback, inventor, and father extraordinaire. He'd loved a corny old song from the 1950s called "The Three Bells." Best of all, he'd adopted me and loved us both—Kay and me—equally.

The nurses said he wouldn't last much longer, but after standing around his bedside for hours, I was antsy to do something to show my love. Growing up, I'd wanted to be a famous singer. Dad had usually discouraged me because of my disability from polio, but I sang every chance I had.

"Let's sing to him," I said, although Dad had been put in a medically induced coma. Kay and I harmonized on "The Old Rugged Cross" and other hymns. Our voices bathed him in love and floated out to the nurse's station. Soon staff stood listening in the doorway, some wiping their eyes.

Dad didn't respond. Then I remembered "The Three Bells" by The Browns. I sang the chorus about God's eternal love. Dad's eyelids fluttered, and he smiled. While Kay and I held his hands at his bedside, my dad began to mouth the words along with me, barely audible.

These days I still mostly sing in the shower. But whenever I hear church bells, I think of Dad, smiling and singing along.

Lord, I'm thankful You adopted me into a heavenly family, and cry, "Abba! Father."

—LINDA S. CLARE

Contributors

Bob Hostetler is the award-winning author of more than fifty books, including *Don't Check Your Brains at the Door* (co-authored with Josh McDowell) and *The Bard and the Bible: A Shakespeare Devotional.* He lives in southern Nevada with his wife, Robin.

Don Piper is the author of *New York Times* bestseller *90 Minutes in Heaven: A True Story of Death and Life.* He became an ordained Baptist minister in 1985. In 1989, Don was on his way back from a church conference when an eighteen-wheeler struck his Ford Escort head on. He was pronounced dead by four sets of EMTs. Ninety minutes later, Don returned to life on earth with vivid memories of heaven. Don's experience there gives him a unique insight into eternity. Don and his wife, Eva, live near Houston, Texas.

Isabella Campolattaro has been contributing to *Mornings with Jesus* since 2018. With an M.S. in public relations and management, she is a longtime communications consultant. She and her family live on Florida's Suncoast. Connect with her at isabellacampolattaro.com and on Instagram, Twitter, and Facebook.

James Stuart Bell is owner of Whitestone Communications and has compiled and edited over forty volumes of inspirational stories for various publishers, including Guideposts. He dedicates this book to Noeleen Gordon. May the Lord's "whispers from above" bring you consolation in the loss of your beloved one.

SCRIPTURE INDEX

A Note from the Editors

We hope you enjoyed *God's Comforting Ways*, published by Guideposts. For over 75 years, Guideposts, a nonprofit organization, has been driven by a vision of a world filled with hope. We aspire to be the voice of a trusted friend, a friend who makes you feel more hopeful and connected.

By making a purchase from Guideposts, you join our community in touching millions of lives, inspiring them to believe that all things are possible through faith, hope, and prayer. Your continued support allows us to provide uplifting resources to those in need. Whether through our communities, websites, apps, or publications, we inspire our audiences, bring them together, and comfort, uplift, entertain, and guide them.

To learn more, please go to guideposts.org.

We would love to hear from you:

To make a purchase or view our many publications,
please go to shopguideposts.org.
To call us, please dial (800) 932-2145
Or write us at Guideposts, P.O. Box 5815, Harlan, Iowa 51593